Nectar of Nondual Truth

CONTENTS

10 Ramakrishna Movement in Nepal
by Dr. Jagadish Ghosh
The superlative presence and work of Sri Ramakrishna Paramahamsa lives on and spreads under the auspices of Swami Vivekananda's great mission, which presently is positively influencing India's close neighbor.

14 Tiers of Causation
by Babaji Bob Kindler
In a follow up article from our last issue of Nectar on the cosmic principles of Time and Space, the related subject of Causation is addressed on a host of gradated and interconnected levels.

22 The Crest Jewel of Jain Scriptures
by Swami Brahmeshananda
The beauty of the Jain Scriptures is brought out here in lucid fashion, discussing such high-minded principles as the five vows of a Jain — self-inquiry, nonviolence, self-conquest, vigilance, and soul-nature.

25 Cosmic and Individual
by Annapurna Sarada
Just as the people of the world seek to establish connections which will be fortuitous for their lives in relativity, so too do deep thinkers draw correlations amidst the wisdom teachings of religious pathways to better our spiritual lives — as is instanced in this fine article.

32 Pavilion of Light
by Sheikh Nur al-Jerrahi
Beyond daily habits and conventions, day to day affairs, pleasures of the senses and even art and inspiring poetry, is that exalted plane of thinking wherein lies what the Sufis term a Pavilion of Light. A Pavilion has no walls; it is open on all sides so that its salubrious Light can flood out and wash over all beings.

38 The Jesus Way of Meditation
by John Francis
Perception of Jesus as he truly was — a universally-minded, wandering renunciate with a world mission to fulfill — necessarily brings forth his natural inclination towards meditation. This article lends long overdue credence to this form of yoga, which is heralded by the seers as being the crowning achievement of a well-developed spiritual life.

41 Overcoming Obstacles to Meditation
by Michael J. Isaacs
To the devotee, practitioner, and adept versed in the traditional eastern path and the goal, meditation is an art already well in hand, but to those westerners for whom this practice is new, a therapeutical approach may bring early success in overcoming preliminary obstacles lurking in the untrained mind.

48 Nepalese Dance of Deity Yoga
by Helen Appell
The arts, when turned away from the goal of mere entertainment, and consciously towards the sacred, act as spiritual pathways in their own right. Here, Nepalese dance is inspected for its visual beauty and deep spiritual symbology.

51 The Awakening of Power
by Swami Aseshananda
Without even announcing its appearance and advent into the world, the spiritual power (shakti/pratibha) latent in the human soul surfaces of its own accord, often spontaneously, and transmits its salient effects upon life, mind, and human activity.

56 Vivekananda & the Formless Brahman
by Paravasta Sam Bailey
In testament to the incomparable disciple of a past Master, and the fullest expression of a true universal teacher of the world in our times, this offering on Swami Vivekananda integrates the qualities of this illumined soul with the the nondual presence of the all-pervasive Reality — Brahman. In this way can the greatest statements from the revealed scriptures, such as *"Aham Brahmasmi, I am Brahman,"* ring true to our hearts, ushering in the deep empathy so necessary for humanity's comprehensive understanding.

"...the performance of just a single yogic discipline is helpful towards establishing a balanced life and mind, but the razor's edged path of spirituality leading to enlightenment demands more powerful tools and methods."

PUBLISHER'S PAGE

SRV Associations - Sarada Ramakrishna Vivekananda
"Setting the feet of humanity solidly on the path of Universal Truth."

Notes on an Advaitic Journal

At the basis of Advaita as the philosophy of Shankara and his gurus, there is Advaita as experience. Advaita as experience represents that supreme place where all diversity merges in its Essence. It is not combatant or immiscible with qualified or dualistic approaches, but rather provides them their place of consummate arrival. Where actual practice rather than mere book learning is emphasized, where religion, philosophy and spirituality are not separate from one another, where knowledge and love, reason and devotion, are never divorced from each other, there does the truth of authentic nonduality effloresce.

Historically speaking, experiential Advaita originated with the ancient Rishis. Therefore, the Upanisads contain the nondual truths of the Vedas which declare: *idam mahabhutam anantam aparam vijnanaghana eva*, "This great Being is endless and without limit. It is a mass of indivisible Consciousness only."

SRV Associations & Universality

The SRV Associations form a worldwide movement of spiritual aspirants devoted to the study and practice of Vedanta and Divine Mother Wisdom. The ideals of this ancient pathway to God, exemplified in the lives of Sri Sarada Devi, Sri Ramakrishna and Swami Vivekananda, are the original and eternal perfection of the Soul and its inherent oneness with Reality, the manifesting of divinity in our lives, selfless service of all beings as God, and reverence for the ultimate unity of all sacred traditions. To this end our purpose is to study, worship, and contemplate Truth so that spirituality may flourish. This is the Advaitic way — *"None else but Self, none other than Mother."*

With reverent gratitude, we heartily thank the contributing writers of this issue of Nectar of Nondual Truth who have so graciously and selflessly shared the wisdom of their respective traditions and practices.

Nectar's Mission — Advaita-Satya-Amritam

In Sanskrit, *amrita*, nectar also means Immortality – and this is, indeed, what we are offering: opportunities to become aware of this Amrita that is our very Essence via the rarefied teachings from Vedanta and the World Religions and Philosophies that appear in each issue of Nectar.

Nectar of Non-Dual Truth is SRV Associations' heartfelt offering of highest Wisdom to the human community. It is the sincerest form of love and service we know to disseminate nondual Truth and teachings which transmit pure knowledge, pure love, and true universality. Through Nectar we are working out SRV's mission of spiritual upliftment and education. And for those of us who are devotees of Sri Ramakrishna, Sri Sarada Devi, and Swami Vivekananda, and also students of Babaji Bob Kindler, it is our great privilege to assist in this mission to our capacity. Please join us; this is a universal movement.

Keeping Nectar in Print

Nectar is a free magazine that can be ordered in printed form online at www.srv.org and also viewed online. *However, substantial donations are needed every year to maintain this publication in print.* Why is this important?

1 – Printed Nectars are best for person to person and organization to organization dissemination of these ennobling teachings that deepen one's own spiritual life and engender knowledge of, acceptance and reverence for all other paths.

2 – Only printed copies can reach those who do not have access to online viewing, including prison inmates, who are a particular focus of SRV's social seva.

Please Give

Use the subscription/donation card provided in this issue to send a check or credit card payment to SRV Associations, P.O. Box 1364, Honokaa, Hi., 96727. You can also donate online at www.srv.org. SRV Associations is a 501(c)(3) not-for-profit religious organization. Your donations are tax deductible.

STAFF OF NECTAR OF NONDUAL TRUTH

Publisher
Sarada Ramakrishna Vivekananda Associations
an Annual Publication
For more information concerning the SRV Associations or Nectar of Nondual Truth please contact:
SRV Associations, PO Box 1364, Honoka'a, HI 96727

Phone: **(808) 990-3354**
e-mail: **srvinfo@srv.org**   website: **www.srv.org**
Nectar Subscription is on a donation basis only

No part of this publication may be reproduced or transmitted in any form without permission from the publisher. Entire contents copyright 2012. All Rights Reserved. ISSN 1531-1414

Editor
Babaji Bob Kindler

Associate Editor
Annapurna Sarada

Production
Lokelani Kindler

Acknowledgement
Image of Ramakrishna's Disciples Courtesy of Vedanta Press
800-816-2242

Contributing Writers
Swami Aseshananda
Swami Brahmeshananda
Nur al-Jerrahi (Lex Hixon)
Annapurna Sarada
Helen Appell
Dr. Jagadish Ghosh
Paravasta Sam Bailey
John Francis
Michael Issacs
Babaji Bob Kindler

EDITORIAL

The current issue of Nectar of Nondual Truth arrives to us here in early 2012 to start our year off with profound thoughts of a religious and spiritual nature. There can be no better way to higher health than to purify the mind and intellect, daily, with words of a refined philosophical caliber. These are precious words indeed, coming as they do from a select group of serious individuals, all singularly dedicated to their chosen tradition and its dissemination.

Herein, sandwiched between wise and heartfelt literary offerings by life-long dedicated writers and practitioners of the Vedanta, living and passed, lie complementary writings on some of the most respected spiritual traditions of the world, all in Nectar-like fashion. And, as usual with Nectar of Nondual Truth, the underlying theme which connects all of these beings and their mature perspectives together is that of Universality. Just as the Formless Reality called Brahman makes up the unseen but pervasive substratum for all that lies in the diverse realm of name and form, so does the eternal tenet of Universality support and weave together all religious traditions. When recognition of this great truth dawns on the human mind, it is immediately free, on so many levels.

Among the many articles which grace issue #27, please find and read (pg. 51) another welcome transcription by our revered Guru, Swami Aseshanandaji Maharaj. On the subject of Truth and Universality, he said: "The subtle spiritual truths regarding one's soul, its past and future lives, cannot be known by ordinary means. They are known through one's own supersensuous perception, and through the words of an enlightened seer. Such knowledge makes one "a believer in soul, believer in the world, believer in karma, and believer in self-effort."

Soul, world, karma, and spiritual self-effort — there is hardly a more fitting formula for spiritual life in the world than this. And notably, Vedanta's noble and all-inclusive nature is brought to the fore in this multi-contextual atmosphere, demonstrating that — what to speak of the soul, karma, and self-effort — even the world can be "believed" in" so long as all that is falsely superimposed upon it due to the ignorance of the collective and individual mind is carefully renounced and thereby done away with. As Swami Aseshanandu used to say, "Renunciation is not condemnation; it is deification." Such statements coming from a man who was a lifelong celibate monk and sannyasin shows us a higher way of accomplishing life in the world, and one that pertains to people on all walks of life. As Swami Vivekananda once said, to Nikola Tesla: "I have a way of squeezing more juice out of my orange."

The subjects of sacred Scripture and Meditation appear often in this year's issue of Nectar, as instanced in the fine articles in the Christian and Jain traditions (on pgs. 38 & 22). And whereas these two principles and practices are substantial in and of themselves, a subtle meaning attends their twin presence. Many practitioners of the day take to either one or the other of these special sadhanas. Those who follow the secret of yogic integration, however, combine these two disciplines and end up with a comprehensive practice that is much more effective at neutralizing karmas and breaking down hidden and problematic samskaras in the mind.

Thus, Jnanam and Dhyanam are like the two wings of a bird, assisting its sure flight, And even though reading the profound truths of the scriptures, and meditating (on either the breath or on emptying the mind of thoughts) both confer certain benefits on the seeker, no doubt, the most superlative kind of blissful marriage incorporates contemplating the ignorance destroying wisdom along with meditating on both the Chosen Ideal and upon one's formless Nature. In other words, the performance of just a single yogic discipline is helpful towards establishing a balanced life and mind, but the razor's edged path of spirituality leading to enlightenment demands more powerful tools and methods. As Swami Vivekananda has observed about the world, "Would to God that all men were so constituted that in their minds all of these elements — philosophy, mysticism, emotion, and work — were equally present in full! That is the ideal, my ideal of a perfect man. Everyone who has only one or two of these elements I consider one-sided; and this world is almost full of such one-sided men, with knowledge of that one road only in which they move."

Finally, as a note of interest, SRV adherents took a pilgrimage to Nepal for the first time in SRV history, and participated in several important events in Kathmandu. A report on some of the facets of this pilgrimage is featured early on in this issue, providing modern perspective and contrast to the ancient teachings which fill these pages.

Om Peace, Peace, Peace. May Peace be unto us, may Peace be unto all!

Babaji Bob Kindler Spiritual Director, SRV Associations

NECTAR OF ADVAITIC INSTRUCTION

Questions from Our Readers

The wonder of integral study under the auspice of "holy company" is incomparable, only surpassed by the direct experience of spiritual truth that self-inquiry provides. In the atmosphere of nonduality, all subjects, and any question, can be taken up, for oneness permeates all beings, all things, and only needs to be assessed by close and ongoing scrutiny of the mind. This simple but surprisingly unique type of inner examination is unknown to most beings, its way of proceeding unthinkable to all who rely upon the authority of the ego/intellect complex for their answers. Welcome to the realm of Advaitic Instruction, then, where rapt inquiries and spontaneous flights of wisdom are the norm, for the highest good of all.

"In a Raja Yoga lesson recently, you wrote: '...a yogi is not one who, through aversion, attempts to strip the senses from their objects in some flight of premature renunciation. Rather, the yogi can attach and detach at will, and this power makes him unique among luminaries.' This creates a little conflict in my thinking when I remember sloka 22 of the Vivekachudamani, (Madhavananda's translation): 'The resting of the mind steadfastly on its goal (viz. Brahman), after having detached itself from manifold sense objects by continually observing their defects, is called sama or calmness.' I began to practice this and found it most effective in controlling sense-impulses. I still do not see a smiling human face, or a mountain range, or a sea at sunset, as anything less than beautiful. For me, there are things in creation that are so beautiful that I cannot deny their beauty, (though if the truth be said, they are only really and finally beautiful to me when I am conscious of Ishvara as the Soul behind the beauty). What I am saying here is that, for me, there are factors, such as manifestations of Ishvara's existence, which exempt themselves from negative evaluation when I remember and reflect upon the shortcomings of the sense objects. Still, I was effectively utilizing Shankara's advice from the Crest-jewel, but now it seems to me that it is being suggested that such aversion should not be utilized. I would appreciate it if you would resolve this apparent contradiction, because I do think the contradiction here is only apparent."

Suffice to say there are phases to sadhana. Sometimes the mind is in a "negative" mode, as in neti neti practice, where healthy aversion, if the term can be allowed, is best. At other times the "positive" phase, iti iti, is active, wherein one is intuiting God everywhere, even in the outer forms. The mind passes back and forth between these two all of the time, in cycles. It is much like Sri Ramakrishna's words in the Gospel wherein He states, speaking about aspiring souls: *"They run a boat race, as it were, back and forth between two of the chakras."*

A yogi, generally, is the type that can forbear the world, even while living in it and mixing with its peoples and objects. But there are yogis who are very ascetic types too. Sometimes it is best not to take teachings so literally, but be more flexible and leave room for the spontaneous essence in them to manifest Itself, as It ultimately does. But be that as it may, for your practice you should fully embrace whatever mode the mind has an avenue for at any given time, in any given movement of its many cycles. Spiritual moods of all kinds can visit the mind, especially if the mind is sensitive to subtle suggestions. Fixating on one mood or mode might only result in one-sidedness, and take away the possibility of many other spiritual experiences ever expressing themselves.

Moreover, the sensitive aspirant can remove conflict via all-comprehensiveness, all-inclusiveness. He must note, too, that there is a difference between immature renunciation and mature renunciation. In the *Vivekachudamani*, for instance, the focus is Advaita, and the nondual state, Brahman. That requires a certain mind-set — or no mind, as the case may be.

Finally, when we speak in terms of a yogi, we are including not just the master yogis, but the practitioners as well. The minds of such beings are at differing levels of comprehension. Even the seers write, act, and express themselves at different levels of consciousness as it suits them, and as the need arises.

"How does one transcend all embodiment and live a Divine Life? Would you say that first comes the Divine Life followed by Transcendence? I have always felt drawn to the path of Raja Yoga. I enjoy studying as well as devotional practices, Dhyana & Karma Yogas. I would love your direction as to the proper path for me towards mastery. Is there anything I should focus on in the interim?"

Primarily, if one can overcome the trials that the mind in maya is placing in one's path, then some huge strides in spiritual life can be made, even in this very lifetime. Then one can join the great souls in divine life. Nothing should be allowed to impede this most crucial of endeavors.

My inference here is to the three opportunities, or choices, that life affords us: we can live a balanced and dharmic life; we can live a divine life; or we can transcend embodiment all together. The word "transcendence" here is used specifically to indicate the attainment of Formlessness, or All-pervasiveness. Transcendence, of a type, is also had in both the other forms of desirable living — the dharmic and the divine. In the first, one transcends adharma, which is life lived in opposition to righteous precepts. In divine life, even such things as duty and dharma are abandoned, at least as the focus of one's life and goal. The Eternal Life mentioned by Christ, and the Goal Eternal mentioned by Lord Buddha, point to what is transcendent of Maya — which is name and form in time and space based upon causation. That is, even Ishvara, or focus upon salvation in the highest lokas with a sublime form as one's Ideal, is transcended there. Swami Brahmananda, the Great Master's spiritual son and devotee, called this the beginning of spiritual life, also referring to Nirvikalpa Samadhi.

Put in another way, dharmic life is a real, true beginning towards the Eternal. The precepts, or principles (teachings), are focused upon, using the four yogas. One takes certain vows and promises to keep them, and has a sense of dharmic duty to friends, neighbors, the culture, humanity, the world, etc.

But, as Sri Krishna states in the Gita, *"Abandon all dharmas and take refuge in Me."* You might have noticed a few of these rare souls, who have no allegiance to anything, not even the world. They have realized the utter futility of works, of trying to rid the mind and the world of suffering, of doing good, etc., (these things all belong to the mind, and can never be gotten rid of so long as the body/mind mechanism persists), yet they still keep their radiant mind on humanity. Theirs is a direct transmission, their help, one of helping others to transcend rather then to merely purify, all based upon the fact that the Soul of mankind is pure and perfect in its inception, beyond inception. While they act as examples, their presence is mere sport, and this shows us what Divine Life truly is.

Dharmic life corresponds to Kramamukti, to a succession of lives lived in inner growth and service.

Divine life corresponds to Jivanmukti, a living liberated condition.

Transcendent life (a sort of contradiction in terms), corresponds to Videhamukti, the abandonment of all form.

Interestingly enough, these three do not have to be seen in sequence, or as superior or inferior, or even in gradated sequence, since some rare souls assume them in turns, depending upon what the need of the time is, and what is the purpose of any particular embodiment they choose to take.

As far as a study regimen goes, and for those who love Raja Yoga, SRV offers an email class that many practitioners are benefiting from. We study the Yoga sutras one by one, using Swami Vivekananda's Raja Yoga text, accompanied by running commentary by Vedavyasa. All are welcome to join in, starting from the beginning and moving through all the lessons.

"The format during your live classes I have attended has usually been free of questions from the group attending. I've appreciated this, because I've found it to be an opportunity to put my story aside (as best I can), and fully open to the teachings of Absolute Reality you express. I feel that the sangha and community has only so much time/opportunity to learn from you on each of your dharma visits, and personally I would rather not have that time diluted by questions and answers. I also feel that those coming to class for the first time should get a full taste of Advaita Vedanta, rather than having it interrupted by the myriad wanderings of the student mind. Am I correct in this view, or can you add anything to it or adjust it for me?"

As to your point of contention here, I am sure that most serious teachers and sincere students are in agreement with it. That is, whereas it is well and good that people get a chance to question, there is the issue of the proper time for it. Again, many souls do not know how to go about this singular line of questioning around spiritual subjects, thinking it to be like that which transpires at social gatherings, or intellectual and scholastic circles. Then there are those who only want to hear themselves talk, regardless of what others in the class are present for.

So, there are some among us who misuse the medium, that is, that the questions they propose are not really asked to get an answer, but rather so that the personality becomes a focal point in the group and meeting. It is an attention-getting tactic of the ego which is either feeling inadequate or, more likely, proud and egotistical. This is instanced by the fact that, when an answer is given to their question, they only pose another question immediately, and do not take in and consider what was just offered. This waylays the special purpose of self-inquiry.

Whatever the case may be, in any given setting, I do offer open and ongoing email correspondence with many seekers daily, and email classes, solitary walks, personal meetings, and other such mediums to satisfy the need for apt questioning. Satsangs, too, are fitting for this end. A healthy mode of inquiry could happen at any of these mediums, leaving the rare Jnana Yoga classes for the reception of full wisdom transmission.

"Would you describe what you mean by 'humility' in the guru/student relationship? While I may have thoughts of my own as I walk the path, I do not feel it my place to argue with you. Many years ago I was sitting with devotees around a master and someone asked him if it was alright to disagree with him. He said that it was, but that the main point should be to understand his point of view, and that disagreements should only be expressed if expressing them helped in understanding that point of view. I would like to make understanding your point of view my sole motive in my relation with you as a devotee. I don't believe that you need someone who comes forward just to argue with you, or even to assert his own point of view just to assert it. I am showing up to learn. Then, also, there is the version of humility wherein a person crawls like a worm and asserts constantly how he is nothing. I could not do that either. It doesn't seem to me that embracing humility means renouncing dignity, but I am interested in learning, the point being to become more fit as a sadhaka. Perhaps you would clarify the kind of humility you expect?"

All that you relate here regarding the ego, the guru, and the disciple, is sound. In the Gita, The Lord states: *"To those of you who do not carp and cavil, I will transmit the highest Truth."* The Holy Mother, Sri Sarada Devi, said: *"If you look upon your guru as an ordinary person, then you will not make any appreciable spiritual progress."* These types of statements provide us with a way to approach Divine Reality, and give us an attitude adjustment — if we need one.

On the other hand, Swami Vivekananda states that Sri Ramakrishna told him to always question the guru, which the great Swami did for quite a long time. Putting this all together, we find that 1) Divine Reality (Brahman) and authentic teachers (acharyas) are not to be unnecessarily questioned; 2) that the revealed scriptures (shruti) are to be taken at face value; 3) that the kind of questioning the student engages in, and that is encouraged, pertains to the nature of Reality (immutable and transformationless) and the problems of relativity (maya) rather than to matters of fault-finding and personal opinion. As Holy Mother has stated, *"Is Brahman something to be talked or argued about, like fish and greens in a marketplace? It is the only thing that has always remained untainted by the mind and tongue of mankind."*

As to the kind of humility I expect, well, here in the West I have come not to expect much at all. Nor do I see much evidence of any real respect for the spiritual teacher and his/her rare attainments. Westerners, in general, unlike the Hindu and the Tibetan, for instance, do not know yet how to see God in others, nor in themselves. Arrogance is thus a great problem here, as is instanced by how we are treating the peoples of other countries. The "might is right" perspective has taken us over, or, as my teacher used to observe, "The westerner prays to his God, but keeps the powder keg dry nonetheless."

Unless and until the westerners wake up and perceive a few luminaries living in their country — better yet actually being born here — and acknowledge them as such, there will be little chance of any true or lasting humility springing up here.

"I've been starting to quiet and purify my mind while meditating, and it has brought me a lot of balance in my day-to-day life. I have started to observe more lucidity in my dream state as well. However, the dreams are certainly not as pure as my waking life, and I find myself sporting in ways that I would never do so in my waking state. I can't say that 'I wouldn't dream of doing that' because I did actually dream of myself doing those things! I'm wondering how to purify the subtle mind. Am I just beginning to notice the impurities of the subtle mind for the first time, and would it be conquered as I continue sadhana?"

Purifying the subtle mind, thus the dream state, is a matter of constant study, meditation, and positivity. Purity itself is a rare thing, as in the case of Holy Mother. Your mantra, given by Her, really, is a great purifying agent. Use it. Go deep with it. And add to it your fondest devotions.

And do not worry so much about the imaginary, even often outlandish state of your dreams. That is rather the nature of that realm. It is not one that you will want to dwell in ultimately, but one to pass through and only take note of. You are the observer; remember that. The experiencer is different than the experience. *"Oh dreamer, awake! You must! You must!"* So do your practices in the waking state; concentrate there. The rest will open up for you in time, by degrees. Of course, there is no harm whatsoever in exercising some subtle muscle in those unstable states. Take your consciousness with you into sleep, just as you try to do in meditation. More flexibility will be the result.

"I wanted to write you because I haven't been able to discuss anything spiritual with the people around me, and it's kind of put a damper on things. To be honest, I'm not sure what to do with myself when it comes to sharing my thoughts and feelings about Vedantic teachings. I mean, it's not exactly something you can bring up to a friend nonchalantly, like 'how 'bout that damn maya, huh?' I know many Christians at my school, and have tried engaging in spiritual conversation, but I always get the feeling that they aren't so keen on finding commonalities with me. I mean, sure, I can interpret scripture on my own, and draw my own conclusions, but it's refreshing to bounce ideas off of other people and hear their opinions. I feel sort of like a stranger in that way. I wouldn't go as far as to say I feel isolated or alone, but it would just be good to talk to someone who shares similar beliefs. I'm in no position to try and teach someone what Vedanta is, or 'sum it up' for someone and then try and discuss it. It'd be like throwing a Bible at someone and asking, 'So what do you think?' I hope you have a suggestion for what I should use for an outlet."

Vedanta is a superlative education, no doubt. It is beyond a mere religious education, like learning morality and ethics, etc. For morality teaches "Thou shalt not kill," whereas spirituality teaches "Thou cannot kill." In other words, death is an illusion; it is only of the body, and even that is suspect.

Until one can find Holy Company (sadhu-satsanga), one has to learn to get by on what Sri Krishna calls in the Gita, *"Love of lonely study."* There is a period where one retreats from society and the world and concentrates on qualifying oneself with preliminary practices which make one ready for deeper explorations of the Spirit (Atman). For myself, that period was from my nineteenth year through my late twenties, and sometime in the later part of that phase I met my mentor, my guru, and eventually received initiation into the Ramakrishna Order. It was a major turning point in this lifetime for me. I wish for every young man and woman to find such a boon. But to tell the truth, this society and its selfish aims all stand against it, as you probably know, or are finding out.

As for solutions, the first one that comes to mind is that you begin reading all the Vedantic material that you can, and at the same time write to me as often as you can, posing all your questions therein. With enough engagement in this process, your mind will dwell more with Self and God, and many of the shortcomings of the world will diminish.

As far as others your age go, the West is not getting the type of education that it needs to be able to produce "dharma buddies," what to speak of beginning to comprehend the difference between religion and spirituality — or worse yet, between true religion and pseudo-religion. Such is the predicament in this day and time, and it shows. But you will gravitate towards, and even attract to yourself, a few of these types if you spend time in study and meditation.

"Once there was an earth-bound ghost who found out that people who died on Tuesday became wandering spirits. Then, every time someone fainted or fell down on that day, the ghost rushed to that spot, hoping to find a companion. But alas, they all recovered."

In this tale, the ghost represents a soul longing for Truth and

> "…. do not worry so much about the imaginary, even often outlandish state of your dreams. That is rather the nature of that realm. It is not one that you will want to dwell in ultimately, but one to pass through and only take note of. You are the observer; remember that. The experiencer is different than the experience. "Oh dreamer, awake! You must! You must!" So do your practices in the waking state; concentrate there. The rest will open up for you time, by degrees."

Freedom, and the people who faint on Tuesday symbolize those who suddenly show an interest in spiritual matters. The fact that these beings "recover" means that their brief awakening does not last, and they merely stand back up like zombies and slip back into maya again. So, "how 'bout that damn maya, huh?"

"I've heard that meditating on my third eye chakra is not advisable for starting out. When I do, and when I do pranayama, I begin to feel a pressure upon my third eye. This pressure does not appear to come from within, but from the outside. When I envision white light to oppose this pressure, I quickly began to shake involuntarily a bit, I feel I am not in control of my mind. Perhaps this can be related to meditating almost every morning for 30 minutes?"

It is right that the beginner should place attention in the heart chakra (anahata) in the early years of practice, and not in the "third eye" chakra (ajna). Premature awakenings can thus be avoided, along with their strange aberrations. Besides, one should be near a teacher when practicing these things, especially early on.

But that you are meditating every day is a good thing. When you meet your teacher, he transmits some subtle spiritual power that has a long range effect, and that will manifest over time in various ways. It will express itself especially if and when you do concentrated practice; otherwise, not so much.

As for pranayama (breathing exercises), do them moderately. Do not overheat your brain. The purpose is not dizziness and disorientation, but centering and strength — to gain control of the prana, then the mind. Do this gradually and with patience, and under the ongoing guidance of your teacher.

"I have been pondering Prakriti as presented at the recent retreat. The Hawaiian's view Goddess Pele somewhat as a 'Mother' figure presiding over nature, so would she be considered Prakriti or Purusha? Not that it is of consequence, since all form is unreal anyway, but in my need to categorize that which exists within my world in order to give it some meaning, I stumbled on this thought. Categorizing things gives my life some meaning, Otherwise, without some order added into my life and thoughts, I fall into this track of 'what is the point of it all anyway.' Then I don't really have much zest for life."

For these types of processes we tend to separate into two categories — the cosmic and the anthropomorphic. The former category explains everything in terms of principles, and the latter in terms of deities. One may combine them, if one wishes, but it is not necessary. Then, you have the problem of differing cultures too, all around the world. There, the language may differ, and so might the intended meanings. But Prakriti being an overall cover term for everything that falls in the realms of name and form, then deities, too, are formulated. In their cases, they would rule over locations in space and time, like the gods and goddesses.

It is good to categorize, like the Sankhya does, like Lord Kapila did. It produces order, and that allows for inspection, deeper study, and realization. One will certainly perceive what is real and what is unreal via its help.

"Lately I've really been surrounded by positive forces and people. A Native American gentleman who puts on sweat lodges has reminded me that everything is vibration, and that we are all expressions of a 'creator' who doesn't judge. I found it refreshing to remember that there is no name or personage for God. 'Creator' is fine by me, but God is also a Generator, an Organizer, and a Destroyer. I'm learning about the law of vibration and how everything is like a hologram set to particular frequencies, as you say, from the atomic to the Atmic, and the law of attraction which essentially states that the vibrations of what I think about will physically manifest according to the law of perpetual transmutation of energy. I don't know too much about these subjects, however, but they really are inspiring me to go into my mind and figure out what it is I want to do with my life so I can act on my beliefs and self-actualize as a man in the world, but not of the world."

Vibrations, called *vrittis/spandas* in Yoga and Tantra, are the secret to creation (*sristi rahasya*). All worlds (*lokas*) get projected by mental vibration coming from the Cosmic Mind, Mahat — the Great. In a trickle down effect, the collective mind, and individual minds, all partake of the power of projection (*sankalpa*). When vibrations get solidified, matter is the result. The five elements are nothing other than expressions from the mind, and before they quintuplicated (mixed together to form an object) they were in a subtle state, unseen by the five senses and going undetected by the ordinary mind. When one comes to know all this via meditation, then the material can be separated from the spiritual, matter from Soul. This is fresh realization.

"Please talk about our 'Home of Peace.' I have honestly lost any belief of what that used to mean to me. I used to believe that when death came to this body, there would be some recognition of being in a 'presence' of unity. There would be

'Peace.' I now ask, who would recognize? What would that presence be? Peace of what? Does the relative not dissolve into the cosmos, wherever we hit, and simply join? I imagine this as the freedom for the body, as Freedom for the mind is now."

As for our Home of Peace, Atman, that is undeniable, and you must think of It and envision It as such. And know too, that merging into pure Consciousness is 1) beyond the cosmos; and 2) not an experience of blankness. 'Emptiness,' as taught by the true lovers of the Formless, is not lack of substance; it is devoid of dualities, problems, and suffering. In other words, it is empty of all those, not of Peace, Bliss, and Light. Those who remain near to It in their thoughts, and with practice, will find themselves in It at the time of passing from the body. Keeping holy company in the meantime helps a great deal.

> "....pure Consciousness is 1) beyond the cosmos; and 2) not an experience of blankness. 'Emptiness,' as taught by the true lovers of the Formless, is not lack of substance; it is devoid of dualities, problems, and suffering. In other words, it is empty of all those, not of Peace, Bliss, and Light."

"Respected Guru Maharaj: pranams at your holy feet. I write this mail to you for guidance. I have been initiated by Swami Atmasthananda ji Maharaj, and have a few questions which you can please answer at a convenient time. I have your book *Extensive Anthology of Sri Ramakrishna's Stories* with me. Since I am not a monk, and have no wife and children, how to go ahead in spiritual life? Which book, according to you, will transform a selfish and tamasic person like me into a sattvic and peaceful person? I like to worship Divine Mother. How to worship Her? I want to worship Her with flowers and other materials on Her photo. Can you please advise me on a simple procedure, and what should I chant so I can pay my respects to Her and give my mind pure thoughts?"

As to your questions, first, that you have no wife is not a bad thing at all. It means that you are freer to pursue spiritual life, and with less outer responsibilities. There is no doubt that having a wife can be an aid, but she would need to be *vidya shakti*, as the Great Master has advised. In the meantime, consider yourself fortunate that you have less weights of that kind, and move towards refining your mind and realizing your Self.

No book can transform you; only you can do that. In order to transform yourself you must lose the attitude that you are tamasic, worthless, selfish, and the like. That attitude will keep you from making a decent start in spiritual life. If you have been initiated into the great Ramakrishna Order, then you need only use your mantra and meditate daily, having faith that the Divine Mother will help you inwardly to satisfy all your desires and achieve your goals.

However, books can help. Read books like *The Eternal Companion, Talks With Swami Vivekananda, Inspired Talks, Sri Sarada Devi - The Holy Mother*, and others. Study the Upanisads too, to put you in touch with the illumined thinking of the Indian Rishis. The Bhagavad Gita is a must as well. Write in to me as often as you like with any questions you might have.

Worshiping Kali/Durga, that is a good sign. To begin, you can create a shrine in a private room in your home. Place pictures of Divine Mother on it, and procure some Ganges water for sanctifying the area and the hands. Place a candle to light during your meditations, and bring good flowers to offer with your mantra.

In chanting and offering your flowers (pushpam), sprinkle them with Ganges water and recite the mantras given to you by your guru. Thus, will Bhakti Yoga become a part of your daily practice. Your readings will provide the Jnana element. With meditation in that atmosphere, the only thing left to do is to offer all your work according to the laws of Karma Yoga. Then you will have a full regimen of spirituality. Keep this up for a lifetime. As the scriptures tell us, *"When impurities dissolve due to this practice, then the seer beholds It, the Atman, existing everywhere, even here in this very body."*

"I am continually striving to transform all situations into spiritual advancement. There is no other option to survive around completely unconscious people — people who live in their gross bodies only and rotate round and round the lower three chakras with occasional visits to the heart center. I am looking forward to immersion during the forthcoming retreat. I have heard about Vedanta, and the ancient knowledge of India for many years, and value tremendously this opportunity to finally glean some of this profound knowledge. But, to tell you the truth, I am finding more guidance for everyday challenges from simple Buddhist teachings. Dalai Lama and Thich Naht Hahn are teaching patience and compassion. I am reading a book by Thich Naht Hanh about creating peace in my life. I know your teachings are assisting in my spiritual growth. I know that is true, yet when I feel lost, I reach for these other teachers for guidance. I continue to also read the Sri Ramakrishna stories anthology. Can you advise further?"

There is no problem in "reaching" for those teachings in Buddhism which bring you solace, as Buddhism is just another form of Vedanta. Buddha was a Hindu, his philosophy born and matured in the very soil where the ancient Rishis lived and breathed. Even Vivekananda has stated that there is no difference essentially between Buddhism and Vedanta. That becomes evident as one studies in both darshanas (ways of clear seeing).

The only thing I can add here is that comfort is overrated. Words like "beautiful," "gentle," "smiles," and such are the by-products of life, not the mainstays of spiritual practice. What both Vedanta and Yoga want you to attain (and Buddhism), since life is ever full of miseries and challenges (Lord Buddha's first noble truth) is a final facing off with ignorance wherein one learns to, or gains the capacity for, taking on all sufferings and transforming them into fuel for realization — turning poison into nectar as we say in Vedantic circles. One Buddhist seer has stated, *"Oh Lord, the more suffering you send my way, the more hap-*

piness I will enjoy." He evidently has learned this great ability. You even speak of your own struggle to gain that quality here.

As for any conflict in your mind on this score, wipe it away. So long as one accepts a single illumined soul as their guru, then all other teachers will easily become upagurus (preliminary teachers), and one can/should learn from all of them. As Holy Mother says, *"The one who transmits you the teachings and gives you the mantra is the real guru, the mantri guru."* Thus, direct teachings rather than just books, and the boon of the mantra rather than secondhand advice, are both key points.

I have noticed that there are several versions of Buddhism here in the West, one which requires and enforces intense practice, and the other which pads and caters to people's comfort zones. We must remember that the teachers you are referring to herein are monks, and have undergone strenuous practice — not in living rooms with tv and armchairs, kitchens with well stocked refrigerators, and bedrooms with comfy beds — but rather in monastery cells, open fields, and mountain caves. They can speak of patience, compassion, and the like, because they have won it amidst austere, even harsh, circumstances, not just dreamed about it in houses and homes. Swami Vivekananda came here to the West with nothing, as a sannyasin, and left with nothing (of the material nature). His peace was in Self-realization via practice, not in fantasies and pretenses about being a great being admired by others. He used to say that, despite all sufferings and diseases, he preferred the Himalayas and a good scripture for his "comfort," and that living such a life quelled all diseases of the body — not running to a hospital and having tubes inserted with doctors bending over the bed in order to cling to life due to fear of death. We want strength, real strength. For that we need to be bold. Let smiles and laughter, well warranted, come after.

"Lately, as I've been looking around, I can't help but notice all of the disagreement that occurs in the world. If Vedanta is the blueprint for most religions today, why has it deviated so much into dualism? So many faiths find comfort in putting God outside themselves. They wait for the second coming, or the rapture, or the hidden Imam, or some messiah to 'save' them. But I don't understand what it is they are trying to be saved from. If they themselves are God, then why must they put the responsibility on an outside deity to enlighten them if they already have the potential?"

Human beings are like babies, spiritually speaking. They do not know their true natures, being so attracted to the world. And so, religion, if it be true to itself, has to cater to those who are favoring dualism, those who are a cut above (qualified nondualism), and those few who are ready and able to court nondualism, Advaita.

Vedanta, too, holds all three, though its emphasis is on Nondualism. Sri Ramakrishna told a simple story to illustrate this. *"A mother has three children. She has one fish to feed them for dinner. Thus, she makes a fish cutlet for the oldest boy, some rice pilau for the younger one, and she makes fish soup for the youngest. You see, each, due to their age and capacity, cannot digest food in the same manner. She has to cater to each one in accordance with their powers of digestion."*

Religion and philosophy teach similarly. Some can only digest fish soup (dualism). Others can take in fish pilau (qualified nondualism). But a few can actually eat a whole fish steak. These latter ones are those who understand that God exists primarily within, as the very Self of mankind.

But we cannot condemn others just because they are not ready to realize this profound nondual Truth. We must forgive, exercise patience, and at the same time work towards educating humanity in this higher vein. Vedanta is the best template for this, since it understands this three-tiered axiom, and moves to school those who are ready for the truth of *"Aham Brahmasmi — I am Brahman."*

"I wonder what religion means to one who has reached the unitive state. *'Churches, doctrines, forms, are the hedges to protect the tender plant, but they must later be broken down that the plant may become a tree'* (Voice of Freedom). What I got from this is that religion is the bridge you must burn after crossing. I'm also considering the *Paramahamsa Upanisad* which states that a Paramahamsa has no need for rituals, mantras, etc. Does that mean that religion becomes obsolete when one has reached this state? I figure that someone like this wouldn't need to reference a holy book or a deity because they are constantly in union with God. Is this where neti neti comes in?"

There is no doubt that illumined souls have transcended the need for books and churches. The thing here is, how many illumined beings do we meet today? Are they common? Rather, we meet a lot of immature and imbalanced minds, yes? If one observes this culture, i.e., studies human lives, goes to school, or to work, watches movies, etc., the one thing that will be noticed overall is the complete lack of any spiritual practice. No one keeps up a daily sadhana. Without sadhana, how are pastors going to become holy, how are churches going to attract congregations, and how are people going to understand true religion?

Secondly, illumined beings once needed scriptures and temples of worship. They would not advise seekers to give them up prematurely. My guru, who was a staunch and confirmed nondualist, still bowed low before the images in the shrine room every day, offering flowers, even up until his ninetieth year! You see, some luminaries are not suited, or do not choose, to teach. These will transcend and go beyond. But other luminaries (jivanmuktas and bodhisattvas) keep these tools, and befriend the struggling world of religion so as to help others who are less advanced. In this way they act as examples for seekers and sadhakas.

So, it is a personal choice of the free soul, based upon character and temperament. One thing is for sure, that "burning bridges" is seldom a good idea. One may need them for returning. Keep them intact for the highest good of all. Even the college graduate may have to return to the kindergarten classroom someday, for several possible reasons — to teach, to test the teacher, to observe his own son or daughter, etc.

Questions, observations, and insights regarding the issues of the day as pertaining to spiritual life may be directed to Nectar's editorial staff at srvinfo@srv.org, and will be duly addressed in succeeding issues.

◆ *Dr. Jagadish Ghosh*

Ramakrishna Movement Grows in Nepal

KATHMANDU HOSTS MAJOR VIVEKANANDA EVENT

The gathering of emulous hearts and minds on 9/11 in Kathmandu in honor of the great Swami Vivekananda and his humanitarian works was a more than fitting testament to the spirit of underlying harmony and inviolable peace and nonviolence that is at the very core of human life and existence in the world, and which no devious or ill-considered act against God, mankind, and true Religion can ever mar or deter.

Sri Ramakrishna Paramahamsa (1836-1886) was born Gadadhar Chatterjee at Kamarpukur, about sixty miles from Kolkata, India. What is the relevancy of Sri Ramakrishna Paramahamsa's teachings at the dawn of the 21st century? He taught no creed or dogma. His only concern was mankind's upliftment. According to Him, there is infinite moral and spiritual potential in man. To develop that potential is man's foremost duty in life. He taught man to strive to develop that potential without wasting time over sense pleasures and religious quibbling.

Inspired by the life and teachings of Sri Ramakrishna, the Ramakrishna Math is directly spreading the Great Master's message, and the Ramakrishna Mission is offering services *"to that god who by the ignorant is called man."* Sri Ramakrishna's life and message are spreading through and beyond these two institutions and have given rise to what is known as the greater Ramakrishna Movement.

The Movement has a vision, as well as a mission. Unlike political movements, this movement brings about radical change in society by helping individuals transform their minds. It aims at the harmony of religions, harmony of the East and the West, harmony of the ancient and the modern, spiritual fulfillment, all-round development in different faculties, social equality and peace for humanity without any distinction of creed, caste, race or nationality.

The Ramakrishna Math is a monastic order of men brought into existence by Sri Ramakrishna, the great 19th century saint, who is regarded as the Prophet of the Modern Age. The Ramakrishna Mission was founded by Sri Ramakrishna's chief apostle, Swami Vivekananda (1863-1902), one of the foremost thinkers and religious leaders of the present age, who is regarded as *"one of the main molders of the modern world"* in the words of an eminent western scholar, A. L. Basham.

Objectives of Ramakrishna Math and Mission

The main goals and objectives of these twin organizations, based on the principles of Practical Vedanta, are:
• To spread the idea of the potential divinity of every being and how to manifest it through every action and thought.
• To spread the idea of the harmony of religions based on Sri Ramakrishna's experience that all religions lead to the realization of the same Reality known by different names in different religions. The Mission honors and reveres the founders of all world religions such as Buddha, Christ, and Mohammed.
• To treat all work as worship, and service to man as service to God.
• To make all possible attempts to alleviate human suffering by spreading education, rendering medical service, extending help to villagers through rural development centers, etc.
• To work for the all-round welfare of humanity, especially for the upliftment of the poor and the downtrodden.
• To develop harmonious personalities by the combined practice of Jnana, Bhakti, Yoga, and Karma.

With the initiation of a dozen Ramakrishna Order monks at Baranagar, Kolkata, in 1886, and with its credo of *"atmano mokshartham jagad ditaya cha — for one's own salvation, and for the welfare of the world"* the Ramakrishna Order has now grown to 167 centers (excluding sub-centers) all over world, governed by about a thousand dedicated monks. There are Ramakrishna Math and Mission branches in places as far off as Argentina,

Australia, Bangladesh, Brazil, Canada, Fiji, France, Germany, Japan, Malaysia, Netherlands, Singapore, Russia, Sri Lanka, South Africa, Switzerland, U K, and USA. But strangely, there's none in India's immediate neighbor, Nepal.

Nepal: Land of Spirituality

Lord Shiva is regarded as the guardian deity of Nepal. It is home to the famous Lord Shiva temple, the Pashupatinath Temple, where Hindus from all over the world come for pilgrimage. The Pashupatinath Temple is the oldest Hindu temple in Kathmandu. It is not known for certain when Pashupatinath Temple was founded, but according to Nepal Mahatmaya and Himvatkhanda, the deity here gained great fame there as Pashupati, the Lord of the Animals. Pashupatinath Temple's beginning dates back to 400 A.D. The richly-ornamented pagoda houses the sacred linga or symbol of Lord Shiva. According to mythology, Sita Devi, of the epic Ramayana, was born in the Mithila Kingdom of King Janaka Raja.

Religion in Nepal is an important part of the cultural aspect of Nepal. The Hindu and Buddhist traditions date back more than two millennia. With the birth place of Buddha in what is now the Nepalese city of Lumbini, stretching religiously to the Siva temple for Hindus, Nepal possesses a deeply spiritual cultural background that is also multi-religious.

The highest Himalayan range of Nepal, including Everest, emulates the spiritual height of the nation's soul. For thousands of years, saints, sages, and holy beings have taken to the mountains, caves, and ashrams to further their spiritual journey and attainment of higher goals. At times, immortal souls like Siddhartha, the Buddha, took birth there to uplift the existing level of consciousness and to channel it in a new direction.

The majority of the population in Nepal is Hindu, while the minority is Buddhist. But the coexistence of these two related systems goes forward in respect and harmony. Both traditions believe in reincarnation. Religion and spirituality in Nepal is closely linked to social life.

Post Conflict Nepal

For the past decade, Nepal has been going through a watershed period of violent political conflict that has claimed more than 14,000 lives. A political movement called Jana Andolan II led to peace negotiations, and ultimately a Comprehensive Peace Accord in November 2006. Elections to a Constituent Assembly in April 2008 resulted in the formation of the first coalition government, led by the Communist Party of Nepal (CPN-Maoist), which had received the largest share of votes. These processes raised hope for sustainable peace, multi-party democracy, and a "new" Nepal — a more socially just and economically vibrant society. Years after electing representatives to the Constituent Assembly, Nepal awaits a new constitution. While the peace agreement of 2006 maintains a tenuous hold on post-conflict politics, Nepal's political atmosphere remains fragile. For many, day-to-day life is still characterized by strikes, riots, political manipulation, and human rights abuses.

There is a broad consensus among academics, politicians, and policy makers in Nepal that poverty, inequality, and social exclusion were at the root of said conflict. Poverty affects the majority of families in Nepal, and is compounded by deeply-ingrained processes of social exclusion related to gender, caste, ethnicity, and other identity parameters. It is known that a symptomatic treatment or adhoc arrangement will not eradicate these ills. Politics will not permanently answer these most crucial problems of human life. A return to humanism as taught and exemplified by Swami Vivekananda is the solution.

That "Jiva is Siva" Feeling

Swami Vivekananda taught that one could only be a real lover of Siva by seeing Him in everything, not just in ritualistic worship. The Vedanta Kendra in present day Kathmandu takes these words of his to the masses all over Nepal. In the words of the great Swami, "*He who sees Shiva in the poor, in the weak, and in the diseased, really worships Shiva, and if he sees Shiva only in the image, his worship is but preliminary. He who has served and helped one poor man seeing Shiva in him, without thinking of his caste, or creed, or race, or anything, with him Shiva is more pleased than with the man who sees him only in temples.*"

Vivekananda's philosophy that "Jiva is Siva" is taking new root in humanity today. It is a revolutionary idea whose time has come, born of the advent of Sri Ramakrishna, Sri Sarada Devi, and Vivekananda in present times. More than a century after the passing of Swami Vivekananda, the Ramakrishna Mission and Math is gathering momentum in neighboring Nepal with the help of people as diverse as police officers, retired government officials, top bankers, businessmen, and youth and students coming together to spread the thoughts of the man now more than ever revered as a global spiritual leader — a true Leader.

Many people in Nepal are aware of Swami Vivekananda and his humanistic philosophy. Recently, in the 1980's, Swami Kripamayananda, a Nepali follower from Dang in western Nepal, joined the Ramakrishna order and is now Minister of the Vedanta Society in Toronto.

Swami Vivekananda's 150th Birth Anniversary in 2013 is fast approaching, and to spread the message more appropriately in Nepal, the Vedanta Kendra has taken initiative in publishing literature and producing inspiring musical offerings. For the first time, the Advaita Ashrama in Kolkata, the publishing wing of

the monastic order founded by Vivekananda to serve society, has published a Nepali translation of three major books of the Ramakrishna tradition. Sponsorship for these three books came through a social networking site and a businessman in Mumbai, Bharat Churiwal, who described himself as *"a disciple of Vivekananda."*

Universal Brotherhood Day Celebration

On September 11th, 1893, the people of the West felt a fresh hope for a new world free of *"all uncharitable feelings between persons wending their way to the same goal."* Awakening to the historic message of Swami Vivekananda that day, one of *"universal toleration"* and the *"acceptance of all religions as true,"* the swami delivered his heartfelt plea in fearless fashion. The hope was that the unwholesome viruses of sectarianism, bigotry, and fanaticism could be eradicated from all minds. The hope was that the realization of the oneness of existence, the oneness of God, man, and nature, would act as a way to resolve conflicts.

But the fond hopes that people coveted that day in 1893 remain unfulfilled today, and the dream of the great humanist lies unredeemed. Our age has been called the Age of Progress and the Age of Science and Technology but it has also been characterized as the age of violence, crime and fear. In spite of much physical progress, mentally man is now drifting apart. We quarrel over God. Man kills man in the name of a common god and religion, forgetting God in man. We have every sort of possession except self possession, every sort of security except emotional and spiritual security. Terror rears its ugly head and violence waits to happen around the world. The present global unrest has proved the truth of Swamiji's prophecy made more than a century ago.

Contemporary science, technology, and politics alone can not answer the crucial questions of our world. The individual makes the society. We, the people, represent our society, our civilization. Civilization progresses with humanity's wise cooperation, not otherwise.

With these facts in mind, the Vedanta Kendra in Nepal recently organized and celebrated the 118th Anniversary of Swami Vivekananda's Chicago lecture, designating it the "Universal Brotherhood Day" on the 11th of September, 2011. Convened at the grand hall of the Policeman's Club in Kathmandu, the auspicious event was presided over by revered Swami Bodhasarananda, President of Advaita Ashram, with its offices in Kolkata and Mayavati.

Babaji Bob Kindler, Spiritual Director of Sarada Ramakrishna Vivekananda Association, USA, also presided with Swami Bodhasaranandaji, and enlightened the devotees with insightful lectures on Swami Vivekananda's teachings. His sacred arts ensemble, Jai Ma Music, offered devotional songs to begin the ceremonies.

Additionally, a large number of students participated, some of them competitors in the oration competition put on by the Vedanta Kendra. A book titled *"Baktitya ko bikas"* (Personality Development), a Nepali translation by advocate Bhimnath Ghimirey, was also launched by Swami Bodhasaranandaji for mass distribution in schools and colleges throughout Nepal.

A Monk's Dream Gets a Soul

Swami Vivekananda, born Narendra Nath Dutta in Kolkata, was never able to fulfill his dream of visiting Nepal and Tibet. Though he planned for it twice, both ventures had to be postponed due to his work for emergencies in India, such as the Great Plague. But now, 149 years after his birth, his dream has come true. His spirit visited Nepal, blessing the entire country — which goes to show that it is never too late to make a holistic beginning.

Dr Jagadish Ghosh serves in a nationalized general insurance company at a senior management level in India. He is an Associate Member of the Ramakrishna Mission, Belur Math, and is also associated with socio-spiritual activities in Kathmandu, Nepal, and the endangered biodiversity hub Sunderban, India.

A Song on Samadhi

Lo! The sun is not, nor the comely moon,
All light extinct; in the great void of space
floats shadow-like the image-universe

In the void of mind, involute, there floats
The fleeting universe,
rises and floats,
Sinks again ceaseless, in the current 'I'.

Slowly, slowly, the shadow multitude
Entered the primal womb,
and flowed ceaseless,
The only current, the 'I am', 'I am'.

Lo! Tis stopped,
even that current flows no more,
Void merged into void —
beyond speech and mind!

Whose heart understands,
he verily does.

— Swami Vivekananda

◆ Babaji Bob Kindler

TIERS OF CAUSATION

FROM THE MATERIAL TO THE CAUSELESS CAUSE

In natural succession to issue #26 and its topics of Time and Space, the principle of Causation is inspected here, in line with how it manifests on subtler and deeper levels of mind, thought, and consciousness rather than in the realm of physics where western science and culture are accustomed to encountering it.

Reality, called Brahman in Vedanta, unlike everything else, depends upon nothing, neither inside, outside, or beyond the universe. Appellations assigned to It, like the "Causeless Cause" would apply here; or if thinking in terms of human destiny, the "Unmoved Mover"; or if acknowledging the role of vibration in the cosmic process, "The Unstruck Sound"; or if considering It by way of acts and deeds, the "Inactive Agent." Many such titles can be given, each illustrating the distinct and singular nature of Reality as contrasted to all other things — objects, bodies, senses, worlds, beings, concepts, etc.

Since Brahman is deemed to be causeless, cannot be the cause of anything due to Its formless nature, then what is the cause of all the aforementioned? The Svetasvataropanisad asks this same question in its opening slokas — "*Students of Brahman consider, 'What is the cause: Is it time, nature, cosmic law, matter, energy — even chance?'*" The answer came forth, "*None of these can bear examination because of their own beginnings, identity, and the existence of the self.*"

And so, this question, if it is placed in a spiritually inquisitive setting, has led aspiring beings on to comprehension of all that lies beyond the ken of the five senses. For, when one thinks in terms of causation, one must necessarily consider the subject of origins. The ancient rishis searched within themselves for centuries for that barely discernable path leading Godward, and eventually detected a subtle "trail of breadcrumbs" which even the pesky birds of ignorance and forgetfulness had left untouched.

When Indian philosophy broaches the subject of origins, it does so with ripe and mature acknowledgment that Reality, called Brahman, is originless. In this way it begins on a secure footing which is already sound, solid, lofty, and well-determined, giving it an advantage over other systems which always try to put Reality in terms of human thinking or, even worse, matter. According to Swami Vivekananda, Brahman is "acreate," placing It in a superlative category all Its own. In Sri Ramakrishna's words, "Brahman is untouched and intrinsically ever-pure, and the only thing which has never been defiled by the tongue or mind of man."

It is with this sterling principle in place and intact that the chart on the next page is offered for study. In formulating it I have stretched the traditional terminology pertaining to the term and principle of causality to afford a wider and deeper view of the subject, i.e., its many tiers. Nothing particularly new has been added in this process, for all this wisdom is to be either found directly within or subtly inferred in the Vedic scriptures. I have only arranged it under headings that expand the present usage. For instance, the terms "material cause" and "efficient cause" are well known to the six orthodox darshanas of India. Brahman is both of these, depending on what vantagepoint one is taking — that of the world/maya, or that of Consciousness.

But in reality, and from the Advaitic standpoint, Brahman cannot be a cause for anything, for if It was It would necessarily have to enter in and involve Itself with divine, celestial, and human affairs, what to speak of lordship, guidance, karma, and cosmological and planetary matters. If the truth be known, however, Brahman's Shakti and Her sons and daughters fulfill this set of onerous duties, the key word here being *Ishvara* or *Ishvari* — the highest manifestation of God with form that the human mind can comprehend, envision, or conceive of. Again, Reality is formless, must remain sacrosanct, should be left alone in its ivory tower — a fact that conventional religion and living beings would be wise to acknowledge and adhere to.

In this wider spirit, both of honoring and remaining true to the tradition and of bringing out what is inferred, sometimes cryptically, in the Indian scriptures, I have layered this chart of cause and effect, complete with the outward and inward directions of evolution and involution, to expose a "trail of breadcrumbs" that will lead the seeker after Truth from one superimposed strata of relativity to the next, each one being more subtle than the last. The purpose of this is severalfold.

First, the riddle of cause and effect can more easily be worked out after such a teaching transmission is gained. In this regard it ought to be stated outright that the benighted or spiritually unawakened soul is enmeshed in the diaphanous and impermeable net of Maya, a flexuous and mesmerizing labyrinth of worlds, chimerical in nature, which are the invention of the omnifarious mind given over unreservedly to unbridled imaginative desire (*sankalpa/vikalpa*). Such a mass of actions, such a series of karmas, has been wrought over

⏭ CAUSALITY, ORIGINS & REINCARNATION ⏮

"The ability to project worlds of name and form, seemingly actual, in space and time, furthers the circle of influence of cause and effect. With the curbing of the unruly mind's penchant for mayic manufacturing comes instant freedom from the trammels of relativity. This liberating process is facilitated by tracing origins." King Janaka

Causeless Cause

Brahman — *Shakti*

Remote Cause

Ishvara
AUM
Mahaprakrti
Mahat

- *Primordial Soul*
- *Unstruck Sound/Word*
- *Unmanifest Nature*
- *Cosmic Mind*

"Inner analysis brings the first real glimmerings of spirituality. In that light the soul perceives the assumed happenstance of cause and effect. In a series of deep recollections it scrutinizes life, even to infanthood, and glimpses past lifetimes. By perceiving its origin it courts freedom." Vasishtha

"Differentiation between jiva and Ishvara is right if one is a dualist. But for Advaitans this notion of jiva as distinct from God is the cause of bondage." Swami Vivekananda

Cosmic Cause

Maya
Vidya
Kala, Desha, Nimitta
Niyati, Kalas, Raga
Purusha

Evolution

- *Form & Formlessness*
- *Higher Cognizance*
- *Time, Space, Causation*
- *Cosmic Laws, Phases, Attraction*
- *Individual Soul*

"The moment that cause and effect comes to an end one realizes God. That is one's last birth. This, plus the practice of spiritual discipline and time, are the main factors in the attainment of spiritual knowledge." Sri Sarada Devi

Subtle Cause

Buddhi
Ahamkara
Chitta
Manas
Kama
Karma

- *Intelligence*
- *Projected Self/Ego*
- *Thought*
- *Mind*
- *Desire for Life*
- *Desire for Activity*

"Souls embody to enact an array of karmas which place them under the influence of the unforgiving laws of cause and effect. Not all of these lifetimes, these dream-streams of conditioned awareness, are founded in negativity. Many there are, masters of mental projection, who wrap themselves in the fabric of maya to merely enjoy ephemeral pleasure." Queen Chudala

Chart by Babaji Bob Kindler
Property of SRV Associations

Primordial Cause

Pancha Tanmatras
Prana - Pancha Vayus

- *5 Subtle Elements* → Audibility, Tangibility, Visibility, Flavor, Odor
- *5 Life Forces* → Prana, Apana, Vyana, Udana, Samana
  — (Inhalation, Exhalation, Digestion, Aspiration, Circulation)

Efficient Cause

Prakrti & 3 Gunas
Pancha Mahabhutas

- *Nature/Gunas* → Tamas, Rajas, Sattva (inertia, activity, balance)
- *5 Elements* → Earth, Water, Fire, Air, Ether

Material Cause

(Chart by Babaji Bob Kindler   Property of SRV Associations)

Antahkarana
Pancha Jnanendriyas
Pancha Karmendriyas
Deha
Maharaja
Sukra
Mukhyaprana
Annam

Involution

- *Human Brain*
- *5 Cognitive Senses* → Hearing, Seeing, Touching, Tasting, Smelling
- *5 Active Senses* → Speaking, Moving, Handling, Procreating, Excreting
- *Physical Body*
- *Ovum*
- *Sperm*
- *Vital Energy*
- *Food*

"If higher knowledge is not already in the soul, then rebirth continues and there will be no other recourse than to suffer cause and effect. Even striving for light will not bestow any real benefit, for to seek enlightenment without the mantra, the teachings, and the guru, is like trying to grow crops only at night." Vasishtha

endless cycles of time by multitudes of beings that it will take some mighty deeds of purification and transcendence for the freedom-seeking soul to see its way clear of it all.

A second reason for offering such esoteric wisdom to the people at large is to generate a healthy hunger for cosmology, both in religion and in everyday life. Who among us that is caring and concerned has not rued the disappearance of ancient and primitive cultures, and lamented as their store of knowledge withered in the character-obliterating sweep of this modern technological age? To bring back, restore, or even solidify one of the great world cultures in the contemporary mind's memory would be a feat well worthwhile, and a great benefit to all of humanity. For what is good is called cosmology, what is better is called philosophy, and what is best is called spirituality. The three are innately interconnected, each dependent on the other in the overall scheme of things. Therefore, a study of a culture's cosmology via a visual, like this chart, reveals the deep richness of such a system, demonstrating, among other things, the presence of God as a living Verity — for such creative genius which fashioned the lokas cannot but have an extremely profound Source — even, and especially, if that Source be Unoriginated.

> "....the benighted or spiritually unawakened soul is enmeshed in the diaphanous and impermeable net of Maya, a flexuous and mesmerizing labyrinth of worlds, chimerical in nature, which are the invention of the omnifarious mind given over unreservedly to unbridled imaginative desire."

The reader can see by the wealth of strata and ingredients listed on this chart that the subject of "causation" has been drawn into several headings, all with their pertinent concomitants. Quotes from the luminaries and the scriptures have also been applied, fleshing out the possibility for greater understanding. These I leave to the reader to contemplate and fathom. For, causation is an esoteric topic, and one that, due to the prevalent customs and opinions of the day, does not get sufficiently aired anywhere except for the rare and occasional spiritual circle of guru and sangha. Even there, the subject is seldom presented so as to bring it into the clear and proper light of day.

The Material Cause

Referring to the chart, we can now look at the many-tiered strata of the causation ladder. It begins at the bottom with the Material Cause, rises to the Efficient Cause, enters into the Primordial Cause, brooks the Subtle Cause, meets the Cosmic Cause, and then merges into the Remote Cause, or AUM — The Word. What lies beyond that is causeless, Brahman. If one prefers to start with the one and only singular Reality, which is most sensible and understandable, then the chart can be traced from Brahman on down. This would reveal how all effloresces out of the Word, with Brahman as the Eternal Substratum, and how everything burgeons into manifestation. But let us start, in earnest, from the bottom, where mankind is presently trying to ponder his situation based upon the triple principles of desha, kala, and nimitta — space, time, and causation.

It is not just in the Hindu scriptures that food is considered foundational; all of life is based upon food. As the line of one scripture states, "Everything here is just food. Beings come into being by way of food. They sustain their lives by way of food. Going to death, their bodies then become food for others — insects, animals, fire, etc." This reasoning is practical enough. Food is also a way of life for all cultures, all nations. And it is for these good reasons and more that it is placed at the foundation of the category called the Material Cause. Coursing upwards, when food is eaten it fosters vital energy and gets converted into sperm. Then it is given reverently to the future mother for purposes of conception. The baby is then born from the mother's womb and, over time, the physical body develops wherein the five active and five cognitive senses develop. All along, the human brain is growing, and when it does, that rare and valued commodity called intelligence visits it (we hope).

Two very remarkable things can be said about the Material Cause: first, the fact that the brain is not the mind becomes more evident here; and second, that the entire contemporary world, and many cultures and races throughout time, believe the Material Cause to be all of life. That is, beings believe that nothing exists beyond matter, despite the presence of intelligence. A detached observer can readily see how an origins theory which proposes that man is created out of nothing, or dust, and a scientific mindset which avers that it took millions of years to evolve the gross universe, came into being and vogue. Whatever the case may be, these two do not satisfy the seeker of higher truth, who must contemplate subtler origins to gain deeper understanding.

The Efficient Cause

The Efficient Cause is nature. Though some look upon it as Reality, it is insentient, so it cannot be. There is also nothing mystical about it, though man, from his very beginnings, and via his ignorance and superstition, attempted to make it so. Still, most would agree that nature is an obvious sign of a Creator, what with its fascinating show of earth, water, fire, air, and ether. But there is more to nature than meets the eye. There is what is called unmanifested nature, but we can study that when we broach the subject of the Remote Cause. What is being referred to here is that unseen and unheralded trio called the Three Gunas, namely Tamas, Rajas, and Sattva. The three gunas, in a subtler form, are actually already present in the Cosmic Cause amongst a plethora of macrocosmic laws. But they appear more readily and concretely here in manifest nature. In a similar way that the pumping of the lungs infers the presence of a hidden life force, so too do the qualities and attributes of the five elements intimate the subtle presence of the three gunas. Tamas is inertia; rajas is energy; sattva is stasis.

To clarify the gunas via example, water when still and stagnant, like a swamp, is under the predominance of tamas. Water, when it is flowing furiously, like a raging river, is under the influence of rajas. Water, when it is still but clear, like a mountain lake, partakes of the sattva guna. Interestingly enough, when we take the three gunas into the arena of potential called the human mind, similar analogies are available. The mind that is dull and slothful is suffering the tamo guna. The mind that is frenetic and restless is laboring under the rajo guna. The mind that is peaceful and balanced is sattvic. Even among the animal kingdom, the astute observer can see the three gunas at work. A dog, for instance, may be seen lying flat on its side, tongue lolling out and flies alighting there. The doggy is definitely in a tamasic mood at that time. But just wait! Soon it is up and on its four legs, running around barking and threatening other dogs, the fear of every fire hydrant in the neighborhood. But most wonderful indeed is that same dog transformed, sitting regally in the sun, neither lazy nor restless. Ah, the sattva guna: everyone cherishes peace and balance most highly.

The Primordial Cause

As we encounter more rarefied levels of causation in the inward sweep of Divine Reality, we come upon one that is obscure but pivotal as far as man's present spiritual understanding is concerned. It is the prana that is being cited here again, that subtle life force which, though so obvious and connected as the inner cause of what people think and do, is never given any thought or credit whatsoever. The Primordial Cause, then, as it is being entitled here, is the flow of vital force on both gross and subtle levels of existence. On gross levels it courses through the five elements, animates the senses, operates bodily functions, etc. All of this deserves individual inspection.

As pertaining to the life functions, and has been already mentioned earlier, the heart beats, the blood circulates, the lungs inflate and deflate, the body's waste gets evacuated, the senses operate, and the mind thinks under the facilitory auspices of prana. And as to how this pertains further to the five senses and the brain, these "six" senses (five senses and mind) owe a great allegiance to the pranic force. Relative to this, there is one story in the Upanisads wherein the gods of the mind and senses, the gods of the five elements, and the gods of other various functions in the heavens and on earth, all got together one day to debate on who was the greatest amongst them. Every one of them got up and spoke most convincingly on how he or she was the greatest power in the universe.

But the god of prana only sat and waited, silently. When all had taken their turn and had their say, then prana stood up and said, "I am most definitely the greatest among you, and I can prove it!" Speaking thus, and before anyone could object, prana thereby and immediately vacated the premises, whereupon all the gods and goddesses present there fell down lifeless. No further argument was given.

The presence of life force, then, is undeniable, yet most beings, even intelligent ones, fail to acknowledge it. What is more, beings who do espy it see its inner workings and thus keep the mental picture clear. That is, people are always and ever attributing their actions and thoughts, and what happens to them on a daily basis, to God. "God made me do it," "God granted me this boon," "God took away my child or loved one" — these are common exclamations. But we have already stated that God, Brahman, is actionless and free of any intention or motive for beings or their lives — these lives (except in the case of the illumined souls) being assumed by the decision of their own desiring egos and lived under the force of their own personal karmas. Practically speaking, prana animates the body and senses; prana brings the forces of repercussion to bear on everyday life, and prana, again, causes the thoughts to rise and fall, advance and retard, aspire and fall down. Prana even facilitates life and death, even rebirth. Knowing this, beings should bring the forces of prana under their control so as to live a dharmic life — as the luminaries do.

On the subtle level, prana holds sway too. This has already been inferred by indicating the mind and its thoughts. These are presided over by what is called the psychic prana, which differs from the gross prana just like gross thought differs from refined thought. And here is the bridge to rudimentary spirituality. If a physicist were to detect prana, and became sure of it like the yogis are, he would soon become a metaphysicist. This epitomizes entrance into the subtler worlds which lie back in the recesses of the mind, as in the

> "...beings believe that nothing exists beyond matter, despite the presence of intelligence. A detached observer can readily see how an origins theory which proposes that man is created out of nothing, or dust, and a scientific mindset which avers that it took millions of years to evolve the gross universe, came into being and vogue. Whatever the case may be, these two do not satisfy the seeker of higher truth."

Christ's saying that *"The kingdom of heaven lies within."* Here, in this refined region, called a loka, the prana works in lightning swift fashion to bring thoughts, insights, and realizations to bear on the now awakened mind. This teaching reveals the distinction between brain and mind, the former which decays and dissolves, and the latter which stretches beyond matter and senses, remaining operative in what religion calls the "afterlife."

To complete this overall description of the Primordial Cause, a mention of what the yogis call "the five tanmatras" is required. Listed on the chart under study as the "five subtle elements," they are another unseen and missing bit of knowledge in our present-day understanding. Knowing about them will inform and connect us to the world of vital forces on so many levels which are important to our lives, scientifically, religiously, spiritually, and medically, to mention a few.

To explain this from the root up, the world, the senses, and the life forces are not to be taken for granted, or left unconnected in people's minds. Through focused and quiescent meditation the nature of each tattva (mutable principle) is to be examined and known, and then connected consciously back into the Self. In brief, after separate meditations are accomplished on each tattva, then this liberating process of internal connections can be undertaken. This art of introspection is mostly missing in our western science and education due to a preoccupation with appearances perceived only by the senses. What underlies appearances, seen by the single eye of meditation, is far more real and vastly more important.

And so, and as a part of the meditative process, the seeker after what is subtle brings together earth with smelling, water with tasting, fire with seeing, air with feeling, and ether with hearing. When this work is complete, consciously, and the five elements have been linked to the five senses, the allocation of the elements and the senses to the subtle elements (tanmatras) comes next, i.e., earth and smell with the principle of odor/solidity, water and taste with the principle of flavor/liquidity, fire and seeing with the principle of visibility, air and touch with the principle of tangibility, and hearing and ether with the principle of audibility. In other words, the principle of a thing/object is subtler than the thing itself, and also subtler than the senses which behold or experience it. This, in a nutshell, is the thorough examination of the world and its causes and effects on the basic yogic level, and how to look beneath appearances, or maya, to behold subtler causes.

How can this process of connections really help us? First, if external life is left unconnected, and all the elements of our existence are allowed to exist in a random and unordered fashion, the mind itself soon becomes fragmented. Then complaints inevitably begin to surface, oft repeated in this day and time, such as "I do not see any purpose to my life," "I am bored and listless," "Life does not make any sense," etc. Here, the zest and verve for life are lost and the inner mystery of existence overlooked — those very things which are epitomized by prana itself. When a person is listless, then, he has literally lost hold of his vital energy, prana.

And here is a second reason for the integration of the physical elements to their primordial counterparts, that being that one can consciously gain control of the vital force and use it for revivification of body, life, and mind. This is called wholistic health in this day and age, though both higher intelligence and pure spirituality get overlooked in the quotient thus far due to contemporary man's preoccupation with food. Besides the fact that we have never seen nor heard of a bored or listless luminary, the control of vital energy will allow the inner wayfarer to access what is subtler still. That is, if the gaining of control over the gross prana can bring good health and energy, and the acknowledgment and facility around the subtler level of prana can open the mind up to the secrets of where our ancestors have gone and are abiding, then the gaining of control over the psychic prana can throw open the doors of the all-powerful intellect and introduce the aspirant to the Subtle Cause.

The Subtle Cause

Higher intelligence has already been mentioned. In spiritual systems and circles, higher intelligence does not mean knowledge of intellectual subjects. Intellect is different from intelligence. The former is a sheath (upadhi) or container (kosha), and the latter is a free-flowing verity (partly due to prana) which shines with the Light of Consciousness Itself. The distinction between brain and mind also applies here. Suffice to say, however, that the Subtle Cause is the realm of mind per say, and intelligence plays the most important part in that realm.

In the chart under examination are found the concomitants of the Subtle Cause, or Subtle Body, consisting of karma, kama, manas, chitta, ahamkara, and buddhi. Taking the last four of these elements and placing them into one complex, we have what the ancient rishis called the *antahkarana*, or inner cause. Just the very name alone informs us as to what the luminaries of that time knew to be the cause of this universe. It is mind. Everything spills out of it like a ripe harvest from a cornucopia. Where does mind get it all? We will have to look to subtler causes than the antahkarana for that answer.

As to the elements of the Subtle Cause, by karma and kama is meant the innate drive of the human being to satisfy the thirst for life in the mode of separation. That is, few know the bliss of oneness with Divine Reality, or having overlooked it in the exciting sweep and prospect of physical manifestation and expression, decided or preferred to attempt to slake this thirst for worldly existence instead. This is like overlooking the real value of land for the sake of its resources.

On a related note, the prana, or life force, is probably the greatest "addiction" there is. A great hunger for what it can confer is at the root of the drive for satiation in the realms of name and form. And the mind will lose itself and give itself into that pranic fire of potential passion with a thirst that far surpasses obsessions with the various allurements of the world. Here is another reason why the yogis strive to control prana, and not give free reign to it via the desire-driven mind. "Freedom from the senses, not freedom to the senses," is how my guru, Swami Aseshananda, always used to put it.

In addition to desire, kama, there is hell to pay in the form of karma. The Subtle Cause predicates that all actions require a reaction. This law is not just a physical one applying only to matter and energy, but is an ethical one as well, applying to the mind and its thinking process. What a man thinks, so he becomes. "This is so true," said the Holy Mother, Sri Sarada Devi. Further, "A ship passing in front of a magnetic hill has its screws pulled out and sinks in the ocean," said Sri Ramakrishna. While this story can be applied to the realized soul's body under the influence of divine passion, it can also be applied to the ignorant man's mind under the press of worldly passion, as over time his karmas tend to pull apart his common sense, and his very ability to reason. So, that karma and kama are innate parts of the mental body, and that body is the cause for all that has been listed up to this point, is telling, to say the least. It means that everything here in the realm of name and form has the seal or the impress of dual mind upon it.

That dual mind, called manas, along with the ego, are the potentially dangerous parts of the human mind, though thought (chitta) and intellect (buddhi), if given a dark turn, can wreak havoc as well. But manas is dual by nature, whereas the other three elements of the antahkarana are said to be open to transformation. When manas is said to be dual by nature, it means that it constantly and automatically throws up propositions without number for the consideration (and distraction) of buddhi and ahamkara, the intellect and the ego. Good and bad, virtue and vice, pleasure and suffering, praise and blame, birth and death, bondage and liberation — these and many other dualities accost the mind minute to minute, year by year, lifetime after lifetime. A mind developing a habit of dual thinking is thus worldly and superficial, and rendered ineffective in reaching any higher moral, intellectual, or spiritual ground. What is more, later it can become fragmented, randomly dispersed and scattered, thereby subjecting itself to be born in conditions which are unsavory and undesirable.

This overt penchant for dualities is what Sri Krishna warns about in the Bhagavad Gita. The dualities themselves are termed *"the deluding pairs of opposites,"* or *dvanda mohena* in Sanskrit. But this selfsame mind, if brought under control by subjection to purificatory exercises and disciplines, can become a portal in the opposite direction, opening to a realm of light that is peaceful, blissful, and liberating. Here, the thoughts, or chitta, come into play. If charged up with this positive light they naturally become buoyant, like a hot air balloon. But if left brooding on the deluding pairs of opposites, then they sink, gravitating to the lowest position possible, like rainwater flowing into sewage drains in the streets. Such are the dangers, and the import, of mind and its thoughts.

As for the other couple of the antahkarana, they are intellect and ego. Much like their companions, they are troublesome if left fallow and unattended by higher Awareness. The inflated ego alone is notorious for causing much of the problems in the world, but its opposite, the ripened and refined ego, is responsible for compassionate goodness. As Sri Ramakrishna has stated, *"In front of the mansion of God is a great stump. One must jump over it or go around it to enter there."* This great stump is the rascal ego. Not only will it stir up countless problems in the world, it also acts as a potential barrier between the transmigrating soul and the static Divine.

As was stated earlier, the intellect is really a key for the door leading into higher mind. It is most luminous, capable of holding and exuding the light of Brahman. If the mind is rendered nondual ("If thine eye be single thou shalt know the truth.") and the thoughts are charged up with inspiration, and the ego is diminished so as to step out of the way, then the light of intelligence can shine, naturally and spontaneously, illuminating the very ground leading to higher Awareness. The soul seeking involution then knows which way to go, and is lost no longer in maya. Even the secrets of the causal realms, what to speak of the Cosmic Being Itself (Ishvara, the Chosen Ideal), are now open and thoroughly accessible to it.

> "...the world, the senses, and the life forces are not to be taken for granted, or left unconnected in people's minds. Through focused and quiescent meditation the nature of each tattva (mutable principle) is to be examined and known, and then connected consciously back into the Self. This art of introspection is mostly missing in our Western science and education due to a preoccupation with appearances perceived only by the senses. What underlies appearances, seen by the single eye of meditation, is far more real and thus, vastly more important."

The Cosmic Cause

Lying between the fourfold mind mechanism and the most diaphanous realms of name and form is the Cosmic Cause, consisting of the witness soul, the various cosmic laws, the principle of wisdom, and maya itself. Regarding the soul, when the ego element of the antahkarana gets refined, the sense of individuality begins to evaporate like fog and mist under the advancing noonday sun. What takes its place is Sakshi, or Witness Consciousness. Some systems call this the Purusha, which may be cited as the authentic individual soul, much different in nature and more real than the projected self, or ego. Even on earth, among embodied beings, there are cases of beings transcending their egos and becoming transparent, living in a completely different state or condition of mind than others. This Purusha is splendid, then, and radiant with burgeoning Self-awareness. Only the fact that it still retains a slight sense of separation from Brahman, a residue of the distinction of the observer and the observed, differentiates it from Atman, its ultimate destination.

The Purusha, then, looks in upon the causal worlds of cosmic law and sees the workings and the secrets of the cosmic process. Space, time, and causation themselves, form a part of those worlds of higher thought. The question is, whose thought is it? It belongs to the Mahat, the Great Mind, a subtle strata soon to be examined. And other laws, far beyond human ones, are present there as well, including the inexorable art of the passage of time in expanded cycles and the alluring power of attraction between entities. All beings, all things, even insentient ones, fall under the press of *raga*, the power of adhesion based upon irresistible attraction. Far distant and below, at the universal and atomic level, the effects of this law causes planets to spin on their axis and circumambulate stars, and atoms and molecules to adhere to set patterns in their own tiny spheres of rotation. On the intrapersonal level, the divine attraction of the soul for Reality even partakes of the enthralling and congenial qualities of raga. In short, the realm of the Cosmic Cause is rife with abundant light emitting off of these specialized elements of higher Reality.

Vidya, intelligence, is inherent in the Cosmic Cause as well. Our chart under study calls it higher intelligence, and the seeker after Truth has been tracking it for lifetimes. In it, and in the refined buddhi that shines with it, the Atman, pure Awareness, reflects best of all. Further, its connection with the Primal Word, AUM, is indivisible, as we will see as this study progresses.

Puzzling, but also revealing, is the presence of maya at this lofty strata. Most beings who have heard of the word maya define it as "illusion." But maya is really only the worlds of name and form in time and space based upon causation. Reality is formless, so anything that covers It is of the nature of maya. Thus, if one looks at this chart from the Cosmic Cause downwards, more in terms of evolution rather than by way of involution as we are studying it here, the entire sweep of maya's domain is seen. As Shankara has put it in his *Vivekachudamani*, called in English the Crest Jewel of Discrimination, "*Everything from avyaktam (the indiscernible unmanifest nature) on down to the five elements is the nonSelf.*"

> "...higher intelligence does not mean knowledge of intellectual subjects. Intellect is different from intelligence. The former is a sheath (upadhi) or container (kosha), and the latter is a free-flowing verity (partly due to prana) which shines with the Light of Consciousness Itself."

The term "not-Self" refers to what is insentient and mutable. The distinction, and a liberating one at that, divides the changing from the Unchanging, the nonessence from the Essence, maya from Brahman. And conventional wisdom takes a step in the right direction when it states that one needs to separate the wheat from the chaff in order to get the grain. But this pertains to physical food and commerce, or worldly matters and their concerns. Spiritual food, grains of truth, also need to be gleaned, and this act of mental discrimination that separates insentient nature from the Sentient Soul is crucial for Self-realization. Once that step has been concluded one can see that maya is in Brahman, as Sri Ramakrishna has pointed out, "like poison is in the snake." The realization of "All Is Brahman" is then not far off.

The chart defines maya as form and formlessness, which brings up another subtle distinction to be made. That is, there is manifest nature and there is unmanifest nature; then there is the Supreme Unmanifest Itself, Brahman. To understand this is to become aware that when all manifest things disappear, as in decay, destruction, and death, it is only their outer form that dissolves, while their inner essence simply moves into seed form, or potential. This has to do with the memory of them in part, but more with their unoriginated nature. This is why knowing the Essence, Brahman, is so important, for then one will not fall into the fallacious assumption that birth and death are real or actual. When a baby is born, it simply appears out of the unmanifested state it went into at the time of its previous "death," and when an elderly person dies, he or she only passes back into that self-same unmanifested condition. All the while nothing has actually happened; no transformation has taken place. This principle is called Aparinama. Importantly, the Supreme Unmanifest stands by, unaffected as well, but acting as the substratum for all that seems to pass from state to state — which is all under maya's domain.

The Remote Cause

To comprehend more fully the apparent transformation of things, objects, worlds, and beings from one state to another, the Remote Cause needs to be fathomed, at least to a degree. This could also be called the Causal Cause. It has been likened to the deep sleep state wherein man is fully immersed in a naturally formless condition, but is as of yet unaware of it, there being a veil of nescience over his awareness. To be perceptive in this pure realm would be to awaken to inner wisdom, behold all that unmanifested nature holds, hear the unstruck sound of Om, and come face to face with Ishvara — the highest conception of God with form that the human mind can comprehend or envision. Such an acutely aware being might be tempted to disclose that all four living principles listed here — Mahat, Mahaprakriti, AUM, and Ishvara — are one and the same, seen from four different picture windows of the soul. Mahat, the Cosmic Mind, fulfills the cosmological view; Mahaprakriti, the purveyor of all the principles of nature, fulfills the philosophical wisdom view; AUM, the Primal Word/Vibration, fulfills the mystical view; and Ishvara, the Chosen Ideal, fulfills the theistic or anthropomorphical view. Other apellations for Divine Awareness such as the Cosmic Egg (Hiranyagarbha), the Firstborn, the Primeval Soul, and more also fit in here, in this very broad, very transcendent category of the Remote Cause.

The Remote Cause, or Causal Cause, is that transcendental location in Consciousness where everything resides, and where everything springs forth from. All of this can be put in terms of wisdom, living liberating wisdom. The coruscating Light of Brahman, the silent Sound of Om, the divine Body of Ishvara and Its incarnations — they are all just wisdom, Mother Wisdom. This Mother is the Shakti of Brahman, She who fashions everything out of Brahman or, She who fragments indivisible Consciousness into many parts. The dichotomy of this is that something that is indivisible cannot be fragmented. Yet there it is, the various universes of names and forms and the mass of individualized souls that inhabit them. This segues nicely into a description, however brief, of The Causeless Cause, which is the ultimate point of any study of cause and effect, of involution, of this chart, and of our very existence.

The Causeless Cause

The collection of citations and quotes gathered on the page of this chart pertain specifically to the various strata of causes stacked one atop the other in layered form. Of all of them, perhaps King Janaka's astute saying listed there heads the row, pertaining most directly to the actual march of cause and effect, and emphasizing the need for aspiring beings to transcend it. And this brings to the fore the Highest, the Foremost, the Perfect, the Ever-free — that which lies far beyond even the most remote of causes yet which infills them completely. This is Reality Itself, untainted by any and all causes and effects, therefore being nondependent upon anything other than Itself. This is Brahman with Its Shakti.

Intrinsically and inseparably unified, like fire and heat, whiteness and snow, wetness and water, a diamond and its radiance, Brahman and Shakti are the twin aspects of one singular and indivisible Absolute Reality. The fact that They are rarely even distinguishable from one another has earned Them the name, "The Two who are One." Like a snake and its wriggling motion, Brahman and Shakti are the preternatural Essence in all things, sentient or insentient. Known also as *Akhanda Satchidananda* — pure Existence, pure Wisdom, and pure Bliss — they are also referred to as pure Consciousness, as timeless, deathless Awareness, and as Absolute Reality. Though fundamentally immovable, nevertheless it is Their quiet presence that animates all things, all worlds, all beings — even the gods and goddesses in the highest spheres. And though there are several layers of causality between Them and all other principles — cosmic mind, intellect, mind, prana, senses, nature, etc. — They nevertheless remain constant, immediate, and intimately available to all sincere practitioners who deeply desire to know and see Them. Like *"sweetness in sugarcane juice,"* They appear everywhere as the true nature existing in everything, sentient and insentient.

Babaji Bob Kindler is the spiritual director of the SRV Associations with centers in Hawaii, Oregon, and California. A teacher of religion and spirituality and a prolific author, his books include The Avadhut, Twenty-Four Aspects of Mother Kali, Ten Divine Articles of Sri Durga, Sri Sarada Vijnanagita, Swami Vivekananda Vijnanagita, An Extensive Anthology of Sri Ramakrishna's Stories, and A Quintessential Yoga Vasishtha. Founder and Artistic Director of Jai Ma Music, he is also an accomplished musician and composer who has produced over twenty-five albums of instrumental and devotional music to date.

◆ Swami Brahmeshananda

The Crest Jewel
of Jain Scriptures

Jain scriptures are called sruta, sutra, or more popularly agama. It is believed that they embody the teachings Tirthankara Sri Mahavira imparted to his first apostles, the Gandadharas. This transmission of spiritual wisdom commences when Indrabuti Gautama, the first and the foremost Gandadhara, after duly saluting the Lord, asks a question: *"Kim tattam? What is the essence of beings?"* Lord Mahavir replies: *"Uppannei va, vigamei va, dhuvei va. Every thing takes birth; every thing perishes; every thing is permanent."* This answer is called tripadi, three-fold, on the basis of which twelve principal scriptures of Jains, called angas, have been composed.

The twelve angas are: (1) Acaranga; (2) Sutrakrta; (3) Sthana; (4) Samavaya; (5) Bhagavati; (6) Jnata dharma Katha; (7) Upasake Dasa; (8) Anta-Krta Dasa; (9) Anuttapapattika; (10) Prasna Vyakarana; (11) Vipaka; and (12) Krstivada.

The Angas are generally in the form of a sermon in which the narrator begins by saying: *"I have heard thus."* It is believed that the narrator is Sudharama Swami, one of the eleven apostles who were present during the dialogues between the Lord and Gautama. He later narrated it to his disciple, Jambu Swami.

Besides the angas, *Uttaradhyayana* (believed to be the last sermon of Lord Mahavir), and *Dashavaikalika* (composed by Arya Shayyambhava, the fourth acharya after Sudharma Swami), are highly rated and widely studied by all monks. *Kalpa Sutra*, the life of Lord Mahavir, is also widely read.

Jain scriptures are classified variously. The earliest classification divides them into *anga-pravista* and *anga-bahya*, the latter being further sub-divided into *avasyaka* and *avasyaka-vyatirikta*. According to another later but more popular classification, there are six groups: (1) 12 angas; (2) 12 upangas; (3) 6 cheda sutras; (4) 4 mula sutras; (5) 2 culika sutras; and (6) 10 Prakirnakas. From the standpoint of subject-matter they are divided into four *anuyogas:* (1) Caranakarannuyoga deals with the rules and regulations governing life of the Jain ascetic; (2) Dharma-Kathanuyoga has mythology, religious stories, parables etc. (3) Ganitanuyoga is associated with calculations of time, duration of cycles etc. (4) Dravyanuyoga deals with philosophy, metaphysics, logic etc.

Jain scriptures are in Ardhamagadhi or Prakrt, which was the language of the common people at the time of Lord Mahavir. Hindi and English translations of the important scriptures are now available.

The Acaranga Sutra is the most important of the Angas. Written in ancient Prakrt, it is considered the oldest Jain scripture extant. It consists of two books called *Sruta-skandhas* which differ in style and the manner in which the subject is treated. The subdivisions of the second book are called culas or appendices. It is believed that only the first book is really old and contains the authentic teachings of Lord Mahavir, while the second one has been added to it at a later date.

Synopsis of the contents of the Acaranga

The first book has eight chapters and lays down the philosophical precepts and psychological reasons for moral conduct of an ascetic. The first chapter of the first book is called Sastraparijna, the Knowledge of Weapons [of violence]. Weapons may be physical or, more important, mental. By these are meant the misconceptions and motives, prompted by which violence to six types of beings is committed. Parijna is twofold: comprehension and renunciation of everything that hurts other beings.

The second chapter is entitled Loka-Vijaya, the Conquest of the World. Father, mother, wife, children, wealth etc. constitute the external world of an individual. But there is also an internal world made up of attachment, aversion, love, hatred, desires, and ego, and the real conquest consists in overcoming these evil tendencies. This is the central theme of the second chapter.

The third chapter called Sitosniya, Heat and Cold, urges an aspirant to forbear with patience and equanimity all obstacles which inevitably come in the spiritual path in the form of favorable (sita) and unfavorable (usna) physical and mental circumstances. It also deals with key concepts like lack of vigilance (pramada), attachment, and the four kasayas, viz. anger, egoism, deceit, and greed.

The fourth chapter is Samyaktva, Righteousness. Non-violence is the essence of righteousness, and faith, knowledge, and conduct, which conduce to non-violence, constitute the true path to righteousness. Having thus defined righteousness, the author proceeds to discuss the concepts of asrava and parisrava. The means by which one falls into the bondage of Karma are called asrava, and those which help one to get rid of it are called parisrava.

Lokasara, the Essence of the World, is the title of the fifth chapter. Self-control and abstinence from indulgence in sense-pleasures is the true essence of one's life. After describing the ill effects of lust and greed, the author urges the aspirant to practice self-control, be vigilant, and relinquish possessions. The chapter ends with a poetic description of a free soul.

The principle of removal of the impurities caused by past karmas is called dhutavada, which forms the subject matter of the next chapter called Dhuta, cleaning. Giving up attachment to friends and relatives, to one's physical body and belongings, to name, fame, and prosperity, and relinquishing all actions promoted by desire and selfishness — these are the means by which the desired purgation can be achieved.

The seventh chapter called Mahaparijna is now extinct.

The eighth chapter of Vimoksa, Liberation from bondage,

lays down detailed rules of conduct for monks with regard to food, clothing, treatment during illness, protection from heat, cold, and rain, as also the manner in which they should behave with monks having a different outlook. It also advises monks, weakened by old age and no longer able to bear the rigors of monastic life, to reduce their diet and finally give up the body while fasting with courage and equanimity.

The last chapter called Upadhana Sruta, the Pillar of Righteousness, describes the superhuman austerities, the glorious sufferings, and forbearance of Lord Mahavir. It serves well to illustrate and set a high example of a true ascetic's life.

The second book consists of four chapters called culas. The first and second culas describe food, clothing, utensils, etc., of a monk and lay down elaborate rules and regulations for his day to day life. The third cula contains the life of Lord Mahavir. The latter part of the third cula deals with the five great vows with their twenty-five clauses. The fourth part has twelve verses eulogizing the monastic ideal.

The Philosophy of the Acaranga

1. Self–enquiry, the beginning of spiritual life. Although the Acaranga is not a philosophical treatise, it contains enough material to form the basis of a coherent philosophical system of thought. It begins on a high philosophical note with an enquiry into such fundamental questions as to who one is and where one comes from. *"Some do not know whether their soul is born again and again or not, nor what they were formerly, nor what they will become after death."* (1.1.1) This enquiry into the nature of the self is stressed as the mother of all knowledge in the Acaranga. It is said: *"samsayam parijanato samsare parinnate bhavati. One conversant with this doubt knows the nature of the world."* (1.5.1) This spirit of enquiry and thirst for knowledge are very different from doubt and wavering faith. *"He whose mind is always wavering does not reach Samadhi."* (1.5.6)

But the subtle spiritual truths regarding one's soul, its past and future lives, cannot be known by ordinary means. They are known through one's own supersensuous perception, or through the words of an enlightened seer. (1.1.11) Such knowledge makes one *"a believer in soul, believer in the world, believer in karma and believer in self-effort."* (1.1.1) Thus the preliminary doubt leads to this fourfold faith which is the basis of the principle of ahimsa.

2. Ahimsa, the eternal law. Ahimsa, non-violence, is the central theme of the Acaranga. The subtle and detailed analysis of the tendency to injure other beings, factors responsible for aggression and violence, and their ill effects on the individual and society, are discussed in such detail as are not to be found elsewhere. The Acaranga forcefully advocates the principle of Ahimsa and attempts to deepen the sensitivity of individuals to the suffering of others so that a social order free from violence can be established. It stresses the fact that the existence of no creature can be denied simply because it is low in the scale of evolution.

The Arhats and the Bhagavatas of the past, present, and future, all say thus, speak thus, declare thus, explain thus: *"All breathing, existing, living, sentient creatures should not be slain, nor treated with violence, nor abused, nor tormented, nor driven away. This is the pure, unchangeable, eternal law (dharma) which the wise ones, who have understood the miseries of the world, have declared....."* (1.4.1)

According to the Acaranga, there are six classes of living beings. There are numberless lives of Jivas, not only embodied in animals, men, gods, insects, and plants, but also in the four elements, earth, water, fire, and wind. The lives in these four elements, though unable to express themselves, do feel pain, *"...as somebody may cut or strike a blind man who is unable to see."* (1.1.2) No suffering should be inflicted on any of these creatures. The reason is that *"all beings are fond of life; they like pleasure, hate pain, and shun destruction; they like life and long to live."* (1.23) All living beings are interconnected. None can hurt anyone without hurting himself. *"Whom thou intendest to kill is none other than thee. Whom thou intendest to tyrannize over is none other than thee. Whom thou intendest to torment is none other than thee....The righteous man who has grasped this basic truth does not therefore kill, nor cause others to kill. He should not intentionally cause the same punishment for himself."* (1.5.5)

"Why and how do men inflict injury on other creatures? In the world these are all the causes of sin (karma samarambha) which must be comprehended and renounced. About this, the revered one has taught the truth; 'For the sake of the splendor, honor, and glory of life for the sake of birth and death, and final liberation, for the removal of pain, all these causes of sin are at work, which are to be comprehended and renounced.'" (1.1.1)

There are two more definitions of Dharma found in the Acaranga. Dharma is, it says, equanimity. (1.5.3) In another sutra it is declared that following the commandments of the Lord is the highest Dharma. (1.6.2) It may not always be possible to grasp the profound significance of the Lord's teaching, hence this statement.

3. Self–Conquest. While the Acaranga emphasizes right conduct, it spares no pain to explain the psychological reason behind it and the need for the conquest of mind before physical restraint or austerities can be fruitful. The author forcefully asserts:

"I have heard and experienced this in my innermost heart; freedom from bondage is in your innermost heart." (1.5.2)

"Man, thou art thy own friend, why wishest thou for a friend

> *"Whom thou intendest to kill is none other than thee. Whom thou intendest to tyrannize over is none other than thee. Whom thou intendest to torment is none other than thee....The righteous man who has grasped this basic truth does not therefore kill, nor cause others to kill. He should not intentionally cause the same punishment for himself."*

beyond thy self?" (1.3.3)

"True renunciation consists in giving up attachment and the idea of ownership or my-ness. He who ceasing to act, relinquishes possessiveness, relinquishes possessions. That sage has indeed seen the path who has no sense of ownership." (1.2.5)

Hence the scripture exhorts an aspirant to purge his mind of all desires and willing. *"O wise one, reject hope and desire [and willing]; you have yourself kept this thorn in your heart and [hence you] suffer."* (1.2.4) And it is but natural that a person running after pleasures would suffer and cause suffering to others.

"Pleasures are difficult to reject, life is difficult to prolong. That man who loves pleasures is certainly afflicted [by their loss], is sorry in his heart, leaves his usual ways, is troubled, suffers pain." (1.2.5)

"Those who are impatient for enjoyment cause great pain to [creatures]." (1.1.2)

"Many are attached to something in the world, be it little or more, small or great, sentient or non-sentient. Thus some incur great danger. Desirous of pleasures they heap up karma." (1.5.2)

4. Need for vigilance. A spiritual aspirant must be extremely careful in his conduct. Lord Mahavir specially warns his disciples to guard against pramada, which means loss of vigilance. Another expression often used is murcha, living in an illusion of happiness created by favorable circumstances, oblivious of their transitory nature.

Thus spake the hero: *"Be careful against this great delusion. The clever one should have done with carelessness by considering death in tranquility, and that the nature of which is decay, i.e., the body. These pleasures, look! will not satisfy thee."* (1.2.4)

"Carefully abstaining from pleasures and ceasing from bad works, he is a hero who, guarding himself, is grounded in knowledge." (1.3.1)

"Thus understanding [and renouncing] acts, a man who recognize the truth, delights in nothing else." (1.2.6)

"He who conquers one, conquers many, and he who conquers many, conquers one.... Faithful to the commandment, such a man is without danger from anywhere. There are degrees of injurious acts, but there are no degrees of control." (1.3.4)

Conversely, the Acaranga is replete with denunciation of careless aspirants and points out in unmistakable terms the danger to which those lukewarm monastics are exposed who, after accepting the way of life, indulge carelessly in contrary acts. *"Some practice that which is not instructed. Some, though instructed, do not practice. Let that not be your case."* (1.5.6)

5. The Nature of the free soul. The sage following the right path ultimately becomes liberated from all the cycles of birth and death. Words fail to describe his state.

"All sounds recoil thence, where speculation has no room, nor does the mind penetrate there. Alone, he is the knower of that which is without support. [The liberated soul] is not long, nor short, nor round, nor triangular, nor quadrangular, nor circular; he is not black, nor blue, nor red, nor green, nor white; neither of good or bad smell, nor bitter, nor pungent, nor astringent, nor sweet; neither rough nor soft; neither heavy nor light; neither cold nor hot; neither harsh nor smooth. He is without body, without resurrection, without contact [of matter], he is neither feminine, nor masculine, nor neuter. He perceives, he knows, but there is no analogy; its essence is without form; there is no condition of the unconditioned. There is no sound, no colour, no smell, no taste, no touch — that is all. Thus I say." (1.5.6)

Conclusion

The tone of authority and lack of ambiguity in the above quotations from the Acaranga are specially to be noted. At the end of every section we find the commanding expression, *"Thus I say."* Throughout we find the injunction pasa, *"look,"* meaning, listen attentively, be an observer of your mental modifications, ponder deeply on what is being said, and practice it in your life.

It is not possible to present here all the spiritual gems stored in the treasure-house of the sacred books of the Jains. A work called *Isibhasiya* or *Rsibhasita*, however, deserves special mention. From the language, style, contents, and the composition of its verses it appears to be a work of 3rd or 4th century B.C., and later only to the first book of the Acaranga. In it a number of non-Jain Rishis like Asit-devala, Uddalaka, Angirasa, Narayana, Vidura, Aruna, Narada, and Dvaipayana are respectfully mentioned. Since sectarian bias generally enters into religion after it is organized, this religious catholicity of *Rsibhasita* is noteworthy and is a definite proof of its antiquity. Its study may help one to get a glimpse of the purest and the earliest form of Jainism, and its relation with Upanisadic thought.

The Acaranga is a holy scripture of the highest order and is the revealer of transcendental truths and eternal universal laws. Every sutra, every fragment of its sentences, every quarter of its verses, must be deeply meditated upon. All are free to dive deep into the ocean of the Jain scriptures, and collect as many pearls as they can.

A former editor of the Vedanta Kesari, Swami Brahmeshananda is a senior monk of the Ramakrishna Order and the Secretary of the Ramakrishna Mission Ashrama in Chandigarh, India.

Annapurna Sarada

COSMIC & INDIVIDUAL
TWO MODES OF ONE CONSCIOUSNESS

One of the more difficult teachings to fathom in Vedanta states that the universe has come out of the mind — the universe is mind made manifest, the universe is concretized thought, or, as the New Age styles it, you have created your own reality. Without a good foundation in Sankhya philosophy and at least a few other salient teachings from the Vedanta, it is quite likely that the student will either reject, fail to understand, or misunderstand what is being stated. The seers of India and others have verified by their own direct experience that the universe is projected by the mind. Mythology, cosmology, and finally philosophy have come along afterwards to give aspiring humanity a way to grasp this intellectually while on the approach to direct realization.

Upadhi – Apparently Limiting the Limitless

Advaita (nondual) Vedanta teaches that Reality is pure Conscious Awareness free of qualities, attributes, form, and divisions of any kind. This Reality is given various names: *Brahman, Atman, Turiya*, etc. It is *aparinami*, without transformation, and *ajati*, unoriginated. The appearance of phenomena is due to upadhis, limiting adjuncts that are superimposed on It. An upadhi appears to limit something that cannot be limited, to divide something that is indivisible. A classic example cites the limitless sky given shape by the mountains at the horizon. The sky is not made jagged by the mountains. Another is the space in a jar and the space outside a jar. In reality, space permeates the jar and is undivided, but it appears divided due to the jar. The seers of India realized *Sarvam khalvidam Brahman*, "All this, indeed, is Brahman."* Thus, every thing we see or perceive is an upadhi superimposed on Brahman. This view alone puts one in step with the seers, for it switches one's point of reference from phenomena and all its permutations to Reality, Brahman, the unchanging substratum of all phenomena. As Gaudapada states in his karika on the Mandukyo Upanisad: *"That which is non-existent at the beginning and in the end is necessarily so in the middle. The objects are like the illusions we see, still they are regarded as if real."* (2.6) In the Uddhava Gita we find, *"That from which a thing originates and into which it dissolves, abides also in the intermediate stage. That alone is real. The modifications have a mere phenomenal existence, as in the case of metallic and earthen wares."* (19.17)

The daily fire sacrifices performed with tangible offerings by the ancient Vedic householders, and practiced internally by the retired forest dwellers, inculcated a harmony of existence that was not at the physical level alone. The elements of fire, water, air, etc., were understood to manifest one way in the physical realm and in other ways in the celestial realms and higher; they were expressions of one Intelligence-force. The practitioner meditated on his identity with this cosmic Intelligence via Its manifestations from the physical realm to higher and higher gradations of the subtle worlds. Imminent yet transcendent of all was the supreme Being whom the seers realized had Its ultimate aspect beyond name, form, and quality (*Nirguna Brahman*), and Its aspect that was the source and substance of all worlds and their inhabitants (*Saguna Brahman*). *"He who realizes Brahman attains the Supreme. With reference to that very fact it has been declared: Brahman is Existence, Intelligence, Infinitude; he who realizes Him treasured in the cave, in the highest ether, fulfills all wants together, as Brahman the omniscient."* (Taittirya Up.) The "cave" refers to the heart center, and the "highest ether" indicates a very rarefied level of consciousness, devoid of phenomena.

Upadhis, then, are to be looked upon as manifestations of Brahman that do not change Brahman. Two of the most subtle upadhis are Cosmic and Individual. Understanding the nature and ramifications of each of these aids immensely in understanding how it is that the universe has come out of one's mind, and importantly, the need to master and transcend the mind. Great sages organized certain of the teachings or principles of the Upanisads and other portions of the Vedas into systems to aid the students of Truth. These reveal the nature and ramifications of the Cosmic and Individual.

The Twenty-four Cosmic Principles (Tattvas)

The twenty-four cosmic principles is the cosmology set forth in the Sankhya Philosophy and attributed to the greatly revered Lord Kapila of ancient origins. As a cosmology, it sets forth a description of evolution, from subtle to gross, thus showing the origins of the universe. In contrast to the western material perspective, Sankhya cosmology begins long before the "Big Bang" and includes unmanifested matter, mind, and thought in its scope. Its purpose is to delineate the fundamental principles of Prakriti, Nature (in the cosmic sense of the word) in contrast to Spirit/Consciousness so that one can recognize and discriminate between what is unchanging and all that changes, what is Spirit versus Nature.

Sankhya posits *Purusha* as the supreme, unchanging Soul, that stands distinct from *Prakriti*, which is both unmanifest and manifested Nature. The three *gunas* of Prakriti (*sattva*/balance, *rajas*/activity, and *tamas*/inertia), which are the warp and woof of phenomena, are in equilibrium or stasis when Prakriti is unmanifested. At this time there is no name, form, or quality, but there exists the potential for them. When the gunas go out of equilibrium, the universe comes forth as an evolution from subtle to gross and consists of 24 *tattvas*, principles: *Mahat*/Cosmic Mind, *Buddhi*/Intellect, *Ahamkara*/I-sense, 5 *tanmatras*/subtle elements, *manas*/dual mind, 5 senses of knowledge/*jnanendriyas*, 5 senses of action/*karmendriyas*, and the 5 gross elements/*mahabhutas* (not always seen in this order). All that we see and perceive in our waking, dreaming, and sleeping states of consciousness falls under the category of Prakriti. The perceiver alone is Purusha. Most, if not all the darshanas (philosophical systems) of India make use of Kapila's twenty-four cosmic principles in one way or another.

Patanjali, the father of the *Yoga Sutras*, took Kapila's work and used all the cosmic principles as *alambanas*, supports for meditation. *Yoga sadhana* culminates in *Samadhi* via practicing concentration on each alambana (cosmic principle), going from gross to subtle, i.e., from the gross element earth to Cosmic Mind. There are seeded samadhis (*samprajnata*) that fall short of final Liberation, and one unseeded Samadhi (*asamprajnata*), becoming established in which, the yogi attains Liberation. The seeded samadhis are made possible by one-pointed meditation on the three most subtle tattvas/alambanas (ahamkara, buddhi, and Mahat) and unmanifested Prakriti. The result of these samadhis is the realization of one's inherent distinction from Nature (*kaivalya*). The Seer is never the seen. The unseeded Samadhi signals that the adept has passed beyond the gunas and unmanifested Prakriti and realized his identity as pure Consciousness. In the higher samadhis the adept attains to the state of formlessness, or dissolution of the mind and remains fully aware.

Three Bodies, Three States, Three Worlds

Another core teaching comes in threes. We do not have only one body, but three: (1) a gross body (*sthula sharira*) consisting of the five gross elements cited above; (2) a subtle body (*sukshma sharira*) made of life force (prana), the powers of the ten senses of action and knowledge, mind, intellect, I-sense, ignorance/nescience as well as desire and karma; and (3) a causal body (*karana sharira*) consisting of unmanifested Prakriti (gunas in equilibrium). The constituents of each body are a regrouping of the 24 Cosmic Principles with a few additions. Prana is not mentioned but implied in Kapila's list, since Prana is the force that energizes the process of evolution. As a cosmic force, it emerges along with Mahat, the Cosmic Mind when the gunas first go out of equilibrium. Ignorance, desire, and karma are also implied as the causes of manifestation that reside in the mind resulting from the activity of the gunas: ignorance, or nescience, results from the veiling power (*vikshepa*) of tamas, which hides the nature of Reality; desire and karma are the result of rajas, which is the projecting power (*avarana*). Desire and karma are what cause the gunas to go out of equilibrium and are the very seeds mentioned in the samadhis above. Thus, in the causal body is the cause (ignorance, desire, and karma) for the subtle and gross bodies. The word in Sanskrit for "body" in this usage is *sharira*. Sharira does not mean a body with arms and legs, but means something that is perishable. All three bodies are perishable compared to Reality (Brahman/Purusha/Atman/Turiya). They appear and disappear unceasingly over cycles of projection, preservation, and dissolution, all within cycles of time, while Reality remains unchanged.

Intimately related to the three bodies are the three states of consciousness (with Turiya as the "fourth") and the three worlds. So connected are these three triputis (sets of threes) that mention of one indicates the other two. The three states of conditioned consciousness are waking, dreaming, and sleep (*jagrat, svapna, sushupti*). The three worlds are the gross, subtle, and causal (physical, mental/conceptual, formless). They are interconnected thusly: The waking state corresponds with the gross/physical worlds. In the waking state the mind is externalized and occupied with the outer senses of the gross body and objects in the universe of atomic matter. In the dream state, the mind's activity is turned inward and engages the inner/dream senses of the subtle body with objects made of thought. Whenever one shuts off the physical senses and concentrates inwardly, the higher and lower worlds become accessible according to the quality of one's consciousness, which is directly related to which of the gunas is predominant. These other realms are especially revealed in the different samadhis and visions of spiritual adepts. When the connection to the physical body is cut (as in death) this dream state becomes the primary state of consciousness, and the subtle body traverses different subtle realms/heavens. In the deep sleep state, the mind exists in potential only. The gunas are in equilibrium here too. It is a formless state of consciousness devoid of a personal identity and associated with the causal body and the formless realm.

This state of dreamless sleep intrigued the ancient seers. Most beings do not remember anything about their dreamless sleep, yet there is a universal knowledge of it and the bliss and peace associated with it. If there is no memory of what takes place there or even the passage of time, then what accounts for awareness of it? Further, contemplation of these three states revealed that in the waking state one remembers activities of the dream state and retains awareness of no memory from the deep sleep state. In the dream state, there is no knowledge of waking or deep sleep, only awareness of the dream state. In the deep sleep state, one knows nothing at all. Who, then, is the witness to the presence and absence of consciousness in these three states, to the shifting from one body to another? The seers realized a "fourth" state that was not a state at all, but the eternal Witness of all states of consciousness and their substratum, who is Awareness — Consciousness itself. They called It Turiya and It is nondifferent from the Ultimate Reality called by different names.

More systems can be introduced to delineate in finer detail how Consciousness sports in bodies, states of consciousness, and associated realms. The teaching of the Five Koshas spreads the 24 Cosmic Principles and Three Bodies over five sheaths associated with the psycho-physical being: physical, vital/prana, mental, intellectual, and blissful sheaths. These five correlate closely with the famous teaching of the Five *Akashas* (atmospheres/realms) from Vasishtha's Yoga (*bhutakasha, pranakasha, chittakasha, jnanakasha, Chidakasha*, with Chidakasha representing the space of pure Awareness, i.e. Brahman) and both can be related to the seven upper worlds from Vedic sources. To what purpose do we make these correlations? Is it vain speculation to amuse the intellect? Possibly, if one's purpose is merely to assemble facts. However, in the hands/mind of a sincere seeker and lover of Truth intent on peeling back the layers of concealment, superimposition, or distrac-

Consciousness

Brahman — Turiya — Atman
Vyapti
(all-pervasive)

Unmanifest Prakriti
Sattva............Rajas............Tamas
prakasha/revealing...vikshepa/projecting...avarana/concealing.

When the element of sattva is pure, Prakriti is known as Maya; when impure (being mixed up with rajas and tamas) it is called Avidya. Brahman, reflected in Maya, is known as the omniscient Ishvara, who controls Maya. When reflected in Avidya it is the Jiva. – Pancadasi

Brahman reflected in Sattva — MAYA — COSMIC/SAMASTI

Identity	Body	State/Condition
Ishvara/God "I am"	Causal/Karana *Maya*	Pralaya/Universal Dissolution *Gunas in equilibrium*
Hiranyagarbha God's mind Womb of the subtle & gross universe	Subtle/Sukshma *Life Heavens (Bhuvah/Svah)*	Collective activity of the Subtle Life Heavens
Vaishvanara Enjoyer through All physical bodies	Gross/Sthula *Physical Universe (Bhur)*	Collective activity in gross/waking Universe *Bhur*

Brahman reflected in Rajas/Tamas — AVIDYA — INDIVIDUAL/VYASTI

Identity	Body	State/Condition
Prajna "I don't know" "Enjoyer of bliss"	Causal/Karana *Nescience/Avidya*	Deep Sleep/Susupti *Gunas in equilibrium Formlessness*
Taijasa "Shining" projector	Subtle/Sukshma *Antahkarana (mind), subtle senses, desire, karma*	Dreaming/Svapna *Mind connected to subtle senses engages with subtle objects*
Vishva "Enjoyer of objects"	Gross/Sthula *physical body*	Waking/Jagrat *Mind connected to gross senses engages with gross objects*

**That one Infinite Light shining, all else shines.
By Its radiance, all is illumined.** – Katho Upanisad

The beginning of Wisdom is calling things by their true name. – Chinese saying

"The jiva is nothing but the embodiment of Satchidananda. But since maya, or ego, has created various upadhis, he has forgotten his real Self." "As long as a man associates himself with upadhis, so long he sees the many…; but on attaining Perfect Knowledge he sees only one Consciousness everywhere. – Sri Ramakrishna

"Physically we must be in tune with the infinite physical universe, mentally with the infinite mental universe, and spiritually with the infinite supreme Spirit. And then we see everything in its proper place, in the proper light, and act accordingly. The finite should be always in tune with the Infinite and that, on all the different planes, in all the different forms of consciousness. One should feel the presence of God always at all levels." Swami Yatiswarananda

"Mind (manas) creates the worlds, thought (chitta) sustains them, intellect (buddhi) travels these worlds, and ego (ahamkara) goes along for the ride and enjoys and suffers in turns. This is the antahkarana, the fourfold mind of mankind, which requires controlling and dissolving, constantly, until pure mind, or enlightenment, is realized." Babaji Bob Kindler

"Brooding upon death, fear, doubt – these are the actual constituents of the veil of ignorance, also called nescience. That heavy curtain keeps a man in ignorance when he enters deep sleep, and keeps him from remembering it when he awakes." Babaji Bob Kindler

tion from Reality, these become tools for discrimination between the Unchanging/Unconditioned and what is changing and conditioned — between Consciousness and Nature; for until one realizes one's identity as Consciousness, one will mistake the upadhis as one's Self and live a fragmented existence. The ability to dissolve the universe of name and form projected by the mind is an essential step. This is best done by first recognizing them. As Gaudapada states, *"So long as the upadhis are present, the jivas retain their individuation. But the Paramatman undergoes no change due to these superimpositions. As the clay pot is not a transformation of the unchanging akasha (space), so too the jiva is not a transformation of the immutable Paramatman, who had these changes projected upon It by ignorant minds."* Yet, on the other side of this resolve, successfully accomplished, is the recognition of divine Reality — Existence, Knowledge, Bliss — in every possible upadhi (bodies, sheaths, principles, states, worlds, etc.) that the mind can conjure. *"That one attains immortality who intuits the Atman in and through every modification of the mind."* (Keno Upanisad) Shankaracharya states, *"The yogi, when he joins with the body, prana, senses, mind, intellect, and all other upadhis, becomes one with them; then by easily removing that contact, he enjoys the Blissfulness which comes from giving up things."*

Returning to the purpose of this article, how do these systems assist us in understanding that the universe has come from the mind, and why is this important? At first and subsequent hearings there is often resistance: "How am I responsible for all of this? Perhaps I somehow created my own little world of action and reaction, but how am I responsible for the entire planet, its occupants, and a universe of galaxies, much less the life heavens and causal realms?" The solution lies in the ultimate nonseparation between the Individual and the Cosmic upadhis, which means that there is essentially no real separation between Consciousness sporting in individual bodies and states and Cosmic bodies and states (see chart). In the Upanisads and other sources we gather names for the Supreme Being of the universe, descriptive of Its identity, progenitor-ship, and rulership of the physical worlds, the subtle realms, and the causal. Just like the individual, the Lord (Ishvara or Saguna Brahman) associates with three bodies, three worlds, and three states. Throughout the Vedanta the connection is made between individual deep sleep and the cosmic pralaya wherein all name and form are dissolved. The individual, the jiva, who has not mastered awareness, experiences "I do not know" as well as bliss in deep sleep. The Lord of the universe, Ishvara, whose powers include omniscience, is aware of everything in the three worlds. He is that Turiya/Atman/Brahman, seen through the Cosmic upadhi, the realm of name and form, who wields the powers of Maya and projects the subtle and gross worlds. The jiva does this in ignorance of its true identity as Brahman/Atman/Turiya, under the impetus of ignorance, desire and karma, and so experiences just an individual portion of the cosmic play — one body, world, and state of consciousness at a time.

It is one Consciousness that plays both these roles, and they are coexistent. What accounts for this distinction of Cosmic and Individual? One answer comes from the *Pancadasi*, a classic work of Advaita Vedanta. Simply stated, it depends upon which of the gunas are in predominance. If sattva is pure, Prakriti is known as *Maya* (name and form in time and space). When rajas and tamas prevail, Prakriti is known as *Avidya*, ignorance, which gives rise to the sense of personal agency, ownership, and separation from others. When sattva predominates one feels oneness with a greater reality; when sattva is pure, one sees as God sees. When rajas and tamas predominate, one feels alienation from others and trapped in what Ramprasad calls *"the narrow prison house of suffering."* This cosmological-philosophical explanation leads to a deeper understanding of why the different philosophical and religious approaches insist on peace of mind, quiescence of mind. All the teachings cited above indicate that the mind emerges from a formless (causal) state, and then names and forms appear. Meditation and Samadhi are the art and practice of stopping the mind from projecting ideas and forms while remaining aware (i.e. not losing awareness as in deep sleep). The yogis and realized beings control the mind's projecting powers and set themselves to transcend even unmanifest Prakriti, the final upadhi, penultimate to merging in Brahman. *"Those of poor understanding think of Me, the unmanifest, as having manifestation, not knowing My supreme state – immutable and unsurpassed."* (Gita 7:24) Om Peace, Peace, Peace!

* The Indian Seers are not alone in this revelation. Mystic Islam states: *La ilaha illallah*, *"There is absolutely nothing apart from the boundless I Am that i am. Divine Unity alone exists, and humanity is Its principle of Self-revelation."* (Atom from the Sun of Knowledge, by Lex Hixon, p. 17) The *Sh'ma* of Judaism states: *Sh'ma yisrael, Adonai eloheynu, Adonai echad*, *"Hear O Godwrestler, Be-ing Itself is God, Be-ing Itself is one without second."* (This is based on the literal meaning of Yisra-El, Wrestler of God, and YHVH as a form of the Hebrew verb to be. – Rabbi Rami Shapiro)

Annapurna Sarada is the president of SRV Associations and manages the SRV publications. As assistant teacher, she also offers classes on Vedanta Philosophy and spiritual life to both the SRV sangha and its children, and in prison outreach as well. To read more about SRV Children's retreats, visit the newsletter archive on SRV's website: **www.srv.org**

SCRIPTURAL SAYINGS
of the World's Religious Traditions

"There exists an unborn, an unproduced, uncreated, unformed. If this Permanent did not exist, there would be no possible issue for that which belongs to the world of the born, the produced, the created, the formed. But since there is a Permanent, there is also a possible issue for that which belongs to the world of the impermanent."

"Knowing the elements, knowing the worlds, knowing all regions and the spaces, adoring the first-born Word, understanding heaven, earth, and air to be only He, knowing that the worlds, discovering that the space and the solar orb are He alone, he sees this supreme Being, he becomes that Being, he is identified in union with Him and completes this vast and fertile web of solemn sacrifice."

"When the corruptible shall have put on incorruption, and the mortal shall have put on immortality, then shall be brought to pass the saying that is written, 'Death is swallowed up in victory.' For the last enemy that shall be destroyed is death."

"The law is not in heaven that thou shalt say, 'Who shall go up to heaven and bring it unto us that we may hear it and do it.' It is very nigh unto thee, in thy mouth and in thy heart, that thou mayst do it."

"The moment that this great mystery has been unveiled to thine eyes, that thou art no other than Allah, thou shalt know that thou art thine own end and aim, and that thou hast never ceased and can never cease to be."

"Human beings who are sovereignly perfect resemble the earth by the greatness and depth of their wisdom, the heavens by its height and splendor, space and illimitable time by its extent and duration."

Wisdom Facets From the Gem of Truth

Sri Ramakrishna

Holy Mother, Sri Sarada Devi

And you think you are Indispensible?

"Let no one think that without him the Divine Mother's work will stop. She can make great teachers out of straws." If a faucet in the bathroom leaks, the plumber replaces it with a new one. He has many spare parts. Similarly, the Divine Engineer [God] can bring a new person to do His work. His work never stops."

(from *Mahendranath Gupta*)

Three Chances at Perfection!

"The Master described three ways to meditate: First, imagine a windless sky overcast with clouds. Second, think of a big lake with motionless water. Third, mentally visualize the unflickering flame of a lamp in a windless place."

(from *Mahendranath Gupta*)

Divine Mother talked to Him

"I was twenty-two or twenty-three when Divine Mother one day asked me in the Kali Temple, 'Do you want to be Akshara?' I didn't know what the word meant, so I asked Haladhari about it. He said, 'Kshara means jiva, living being; Akshara means Paramatman, the Supreme Soul.'"

(from *The Gospel of Sri Ramakrishna*)

Money makes the world go Round....or not

"Lust and greed alone is the world. Many people regard money as their very life-blood. But however much you may show love for money, one day, perhaps, every bit of it will slip through your hand. They alone make good use of their money who spend it for the worship of God and the service of holy men and the devotees. Their money bears fruit, not those who make their living by trafficking in human suffering."

(from *The Gospel of Sri Ramakrishna*)

The Final Resort in this World

"Misery is inevitable for an embodied being; even the creator has no power to stop it. If you want peace, practice spiritual disciplines."

(from *Mahendranath Gupta*)

When Nondiscrimination Works!

"There is no certainty when death will come, so it is better to visit holy places soon without discriminating between auspicious or inauspicious times."

(from *Mahendranath Gupta*)

Karmic Hygiene

"I eat through the mouths of all of you, my dears. Your eating is as good as my taking food. How much I have eaten since coming to the circle of the Master. But you should know that there are certain dangers involved in eating together with others from the same plate, in lying on the same bed with another, and in using someone else's cloth or bath towel. Also, a person's good or bad physical condition may be transferred to the body of another. Therefore be careful. My child, your body is also my body. I suffer if you do not keep good health."

(from the *Sri Sarada Vijnanagita*)

Brahmarpanam.....

"Eating food that has not been offered to God is equivalent to eating sin. The place and manner in which it is prepared is also important. So first, offer to God whatever you eat. One must not eat unoffered food. As your food is, so will be your blood. From pure food you will get pure blood, pure mind, and pure strength. Pure mind begets prema, ecstatic love for God."

(from the *Sri Sarada Vijnanagita*)

Wisdom Facets From the Gem of Truth

Painting by Swami Tadatmananda

Swami Vivekananda | Sri Ramakrishna's Disciples & Devotees

Universality at Work

"If anyone here hopes that this unity will come by the triumph of any one of the religions and the destruction of the others, to him I say, 'Brother, yours is an impossible hope.' Do I wish that the Christian would become a Hindu? God forbid. Do I wish that the Hindu or Buddhist would become Christian? God forbid. The Christian is not to become a Hindu or a Buddhist, nor a Hindu or a Buddhist to become a Christian. But each must assimilate the spirit of the others and yet preserve his individuality and grow according to his own law of growth."

(from *Mahendranath Gupta*)

Asato ma sad gamaya....

"Why does a Christian go to Church? Why is the Cross holy? Why is the face turned towards the sky in prayers? Why are there so many images in the Catholic Church? Why are there so many images in the minds of Protestants when they pray? My brethren, we can no more think about anything without a mental image than we can live without breathing....If a man can realize his divine nature with the help of an image, would it be right to call that a sin? Nor even when he has passed that stage, should he call it an error? To the Hindu, man is not travelling from error to truth, but from truth to truth, from lower to higher truth."

(from *Mahendranath Gupta*)

Seeing Through Maya

"This world is and is not, manifold yet one. I shall unravel its mystery, and I shall know whether grief be there or anything else; I do not flee from it as from a bugbear. I will know all about it. As to the infinite pain that attends its search, I am embracing it in its fullest measure. Am I a beast that you frighten me with happiness and misery, decay and death, which are but the outcome of the senses? I will know about it — give up my life for it."

(from *The Complete Works* & *Vivekananda Vijnanagita*)

Mankind, Maya, and Manipulation

"What a watchful eye the Master had! He did not miss any detail. Once a disciple paid a pice for six betel leaves instead of ten. Immediately the Master scolded him: 'Why do you allow yourself to be cheated? You must get the right quantity. If there is any extra amount offered, take it to distribute among others. But by no means be cheated.' This saying of the Master's has a deep significance. If a person is not careful, maya will use lust and gold to cheat him. Some people are heedless and develop a personality that permits them to be cheated by others."

(from *Mahendranath Gupta*)

Where Education seeks Enlightenment

"Two aspects we learn from Mother's life: (1) Brahmacharya and absorption in God, (2) Self-control and service. She did not know anything other than God. Seeing God in every being, she served Him day and night. All her teachings are mantras. Many highly educated women, including Nivedita, would sit at her feet with folded hands. Modern ideas and education were subordinate to her towering personality."

(from *Mahendranath Gupta*)

You do the Math!

"The ideal of the Math is the Master, the Avatara – indivisible Satchidananda – who came as a human being. The monks perform various works – worship of the Master, and relief, hospital, publication, educational work – as service to the Master. The whole atmosphere of the monastery is permeated with spirituality."

(from *Mahendranath Gupta*)

Then Die, Desire.....

"Samadhi is the natural state of all human beings, but it seems to be unnatural. Why? Because of our craving for worldly enjoyment. When desires cease, Samadhi begins."

(from *Mahendranath Gupta*)

◆ *Sheikh Nur Al-Jerrahi*

PAVILION OF LIGHT

"A Pavilion of Light: it is an opening. It has no walls; it is open to the landscape, it is open to infinity."

On March 3rd, 1994, on the 21st day of Ramadan, at the Masjid al-Farah, Sheikh Nur Al-Jerrahi gave out this most profound and endearing teaching on the Pavilion of Light to the Sufis gathered near him.

Sheikh Nur: May the prayer come forth from Allah. May we pray through the human heart and mind and may we direct it only to Allah who is the sole Source and Goal of Being. Most precious Allah, You are the Reality, You are the Witness to the Reality, You are the Constituter of prophecy. You are the One who sends the prophets to call Yourself back to Yourself.

Most precious Allah, lead us through the seven levels of religion, each level more beautiful, more profound. Give us the longing heart that is necessary to ascend from one level to the next. May we cry with longing in the midnight hour. May we spend our days considering more and more deeply the profound principles of Islam. May our very breath become the vehicle for the Divine Names. May we gradually totally purify and totally open our entire being to You and only to You.

Most precious Allah, You have beautified this planet with the advent of Prophet Muhammad, *Salallahu alayhi wa sallim*. You have beautified this planet with his community of lovers, may Allah always be pleased with them. They are the representatives of the prophetic teaching which has come from time immemorial — one single essential teaching which is to turn around completely towards your own true Source and make your limited life an offering into the Limitless Life. May we have that taste of the Limitless Life. May it shine through us as the *tawhid*, as the Divine Unity. May we feel it in our perception, in our thinking. May we touch each other and help each other with this feeling of unity — not with emotions, not with belief systems, not with ideological attitudes of any kind. May we be motivated from the very depth of our being by the Divine Unity. May the only sweetness of our life be the expression of that unity. Amin, Amin, Ya Rabbi-l-'alamin. Alhamdulillahi Rabbi-l-alamin. Al-Fatiha.

Ya Hazreti Ali, Ya Hazreti Ali, Ya Hazreti Ali… Ya Hazreti Fatima, Hazreti Hassan, Hazreti Hussain, Ya Sultan Abu Bakr Siddiq, Umar, Hazreti Uthman, Ya Bayazid Bistami, Ya Junayd-i-Baghdadi, Ya Hazreti Abdul Qadir Gaylani, Ibrahim Dusuqi, Ya Hazreti Jelaluddin Rumi, Ya Shems-i-Tabrizi, Ya Rabia al-Adawiya, Ya Mansur al-Hallaj, Ya Shah Naqshiband, Ya Muinuddin Chishti, Ya Sultan Muhammad Nureddin Jerrahi, the one who has gathered the tariqas together into the principle of tariqa which is a flame that has infinite facets, infinite phases; Ya Sultan Muzaffer Ashqi al-Jerrahi, the emir of love to Western humanity; Ya Sultan Allah, Hu… *As-salam 'alaykum*.

Sheikh Nur: Right now an unveiling is going on, and one can see, during the Ramadan, this unveiling process intensifying. Here in this room this evening you can see the beautiful results of the unveiling. Whatever perfection is here in this room is being manifested from inside of our souls.

Visitor: How would you describe the character of our soul?

Sheikh Nur: The soul is that essential part of ourselves that was created before time, so it is not exactly our character. Our character grows out of our soul, but the soul is a pure radiant reality that is really indescribable. It is one of Allah's mysteries because Allah breathed His breath into that soul. He breathed His Essence into that soul. Just as Allah is indescribable, in a certain way the soul is indescribable. Then we have the seven levels of the nafs, of the limited self, which surround that soul.

Forgive me for making pictures of it, because this is not something that ultimately can be pictured. Taking it as a metaphor, the soul is this pure light which came out of the Nur Muhammad, *Salallahu alayhi wa sallim*. It came out of this original first light from which all of the souls were created. In the center is that original light and surrounding it are these seven more limiting factors. The biological form is connected with the al-nafs al-ammara, the most outward sphere of the self. If we didn't have that we would stop breathing when we went to sleep at night. This most limited self is what holds us to life and what causes us, if we are drowning, to fight to live.

Visitor: So the soul is actually infinite?

Sheikh Nur: The soul itself is actually infinite, and Allah hints at that in many ways in the Hadith. He says in a hadith Qudsi: *"I, Allah, who cannot fit into the entire creation, can fit into the heart of the believer."* That implies the infinite. The word heart is used, but the word soul could have been used too — synonymous here, in a sense. It is a very beautiful point that you are bringing out — the infinite nature of the human soul.

Visitor: Some people use the expression, "I didn't ask to be in this world," but in scripture it says that we asked to be here.

Sheikh Nur: According to Quran, we definitely asked to be here. Allah was going to create the souls anyway. That is His infinite power and His infinite creativity that we don't ask questions about. But He gave us the choice, *"Do you want to be here like an ant or a bird is here, or do you want to be here as a human being?"* We said, *"We want to be here as human beings. We want to have freedom and we want to consciously strive to return into our Source."* So our freedom, our conscious striving, everything that causes us to be human, we definitely asked for. And we took a huge responsibility. In Quran it says that Allah offered this responsibility to the mountains and they didn't accept. He finally offered it to humanity, and humanity, although its vehicle was imperfect (the soul was perfect, but the vehicle of the society and culture is imperfect), accepted that great responsibility. We have all accepted the most profound responsibility from Allah Most High. We definitely asked for it. When we get here the veiling process begins to occur and we forget about that responsibility and we make absurd statements like, "No one ever asked me to come here, why am I here?" I call that existential angst. People get into the basic anxiety. The most dangerous thing is to follow your own subjective impulses, like doubt, and to turn away from the genuine guidance that has been given to humanity. If someone says, "I question why I am here. No one asked me if I wanted to be here," that is pure subjective thinking. If they would just simply turn to Quran or any of the other revealed books, there would be ample evidence of why we are here. We are here for the greatest significant reason. We have accepted a vast responsibility from Allah, and we have the strength.

Visitor: What does it mean that the human being was created in the Divine image?

Sheikh Nur: It is obviously not an image like you would see in a mirror. Image in this case, means basic nature. Allah created human beings as a bearer of His Essence, as a bearer of His True Nature. He didn't create any other being in exactly that way. They are reflections. Even the Archangel Gabriel, *'alayhi salam*, could not go with Rasulallah, upon him be peace, across the Lote Tree of the Far Boundary into the Garden of Essence. He said, *"Ya Rasulallah, I have to stay here. Only you can go there because your homeland is the Divine Essence."* The human being alone has been created in this Divine Image. By image we do not mean something like a form, because Allah is formless, but we have been created with that essential kinship with Divine Reality. Allah calls His Prophet Habibullah, My beloved one. All of humanity could have that title. All of humanity could be called Habibullah, the beloved of Allah. You don't love someone that intensely unless they belong to you, are from your very own being — unless they have that inner relationship to you. We have to think about this: the nature of the human being is very, very unique — very, very special.

The beautiful thing is that we have already lived up to that responsibility. From before eternity we said "Yes." We don't have to have an inferiority complex about being here: 'Well, I don't know if I can really be Muslim, I don't know if I can really be upright." We have already made the commitment, and Allah, *Inshallah*, will accept our intention. Now we have to fight the greater jihad with all the levels of veils which Allah permits us. Allah said to His Prophet Adam, *"Enter with your noble wife into the veils of time."* This entering into the veils was also part of the Divine Plan. The first ones who entered in were our beloved mother and father of the original human beings, and they became the first light of prophecy. We don't look upon them as fallen creatures; we look upon Adam and Eve, *alayhi salam*, as very enlightened prophetic beings. Their descent into the veils was something that Allah had already foreordained. We don't even complain to Allah about the imperfection of our society and our family, because these are the veils and Allah sent us into the veils in order that we could unveil His love. So even the veils we don't complain about.

That was a beautiful inquiry, thank you. Does anyone else have a question about the basic nature of humanity? It seems like we should start here because one might say, "Well, let's look into the basic nature of Allah," but who knows the basic nature of Allah? Here we are as human beings — presumably we should know what humanity is! We should start here and by knowing this we will find Allah. Rasulallah says, *"The one who knows himself knows His Lord."* If we really know our basic structure then we will understand how it relates intimately to the Being of the Creator.

Visitor: I have a question, but it is on a different subject.

Sheikh Nur: That's okay, we are open.

Visitor: I came here a few months ago and you talked to me about fear of God, and told me not to be scared.

Sheikh Nur: I remember you!

Visitor: I didn't really understand it until I started to really think about it. Since then I have been really terrified when I think about the power that is there. Even as I speak the words now I am touching into that fear.

Sheikh Nur: That is the best way. I told him, "Don't be scared of Allah," so now he thinks about how beautiful, how amazing Allah is, and that one shouldn't be scared of him. Then he gets true awe, true fear, which is like a sacred fear. It is not like a neurotic type of fear that is imposed by some societal force: "You will get a punishment if you do this.'" You are tasting the real thing. I am so glad.

Visitor: The fear seems to cut through everything. Everything that is talked about, or discussed, or the interactions I have with people seem to be noise in a certain way. I guess it is the fear that inspires me, and the fear of the trials that I have to face while I am on earth that has kept me from coming back here. I have been scared to come back all this time.

Sheikh Nur: Welcome! *as-salam alaykum!* You belong to this community inwardly, but there is a period of testing and staying away, and that is all right too. Allah repeatedly calls us. It is not wrong to try to avoid Allah, because then you find out that you can't avoid Him. Otherwise you might think that it is your choice to come here, that it is your choice to be a submitted person. You might think you were doing it for Allah, whereas Quran says that Allah doesn't need the submission of any being. It is all right to take the approach that you have been taking because now you know that you are here by the Divine Power, and you will come to know that more and more. All of us know that. That is what makes a community like this so beautiful. We don't have a conventional religion; we are not here because anyone is going to see us here. We don't have any reason to be here except that the Divine Power brings us here. Everyone who comes in this door we accept on that basis — the Divine Power brings them.

Dervish Saki (seven years old): What happens when you die? Do you come back to earth?

Sheikh Nur: Saki, when you die, you go into the Divine Heart. You go into the Heart of Allah. No one knows all of the beautiful things that are there. Quran says, *"You receive everything that you want or need and there is always more."* There is always more. Inside that Divine Heart there is everything: there is earth, there are angels, there is the whole creation, there is your mother. Everything is inside that Divine Heart, so you won't be separated from anything. You won't necessarily have to come back anyplace — everything will be there in that Heart. When you are there, for instance, you can pray for earth, you can help earth. I hope I meet you there someday, *Inshallah*.

Dervish Bedriya: Sheikh Nur, when the soul leaves the body, how does it travel?

Sheikh Nur: In a garment of light. In a garment of light. But when it removes that garment then it is in its pure nature. Then it is with Allah in the most intimate manner. Depending on the level of the evolution, that is experienced as beautiful gardens, as streams of peace, and beautiful youths, and banquet tables. As one matures and one says, "O Allah, I only want Your Good Pleasure." Then that imagery may disappear and something even greater will be shown. As our brother said, Allah leads us from level to level.

(To Visitor) What He showed you was the fear of Him. *Alhamdulillah*, He brought you back into the straight path. Now He is going to continue to show you things, *Inshallah*. He is going to show you His Love, He is going to show you His Beauty, His Gifts. He is going to show you His Tenderness, *Inshallah*, gradually. All of us are like children in school. We are going from grade to grade, from class to class. In first or second grade you have got to threaten the kids to get them to do anything. Maybe you have to threaten them all the way through to a certain level, but then at a certain point they love to be in the school and they see the school in an entirely different way. They are not afraid of the teacher anymore as they realize the teacher was just threatening them because they were unruly little children. They realize that the teacher is actually a very wise — an infinitely wise being that doesn't have to threaten anymore. Then an intimate friendship develops. Then the soul begins doing research in the Divine Attributes, in the "library" of the Divine Attributes, you might say. The soul does its own research and discovers unique beauties, Divine Mysteries. That is what we are involved in here. You have been welcomed by Allah into a circle of people who are doing research in the Divine Attributes. We are not afraid of the teacher at all. We have intimate friendship with Allah Most High. Welcome into that kind of an atmosphere. All of us are here because of Allah's good pleasure with us. All of us are very honored to be here in this room, in this companionship.

Visitor: I am not really concerned at all about where I have been before, or where I am going afterwards, because I am here now. The more deeply I look at the earth around me and at the city I am living in, the more I feel that there is a very ill wind blowing, I see so much hatred and so much pain.

Sheikh Nur: I have to inform you about something. You are looking at the surface of the ocean. You have to look at the depths of the ocean too. I am not saying that your perception of the surface is wrong, but there is a depth to the ocean. You said that you are not concerned with where you were before or where you are going, because, as you said, "I am here now." The question is, where are you now? That is a very good question. Where are we now, really? In truth, where are we? That is a very profound question. We are, first of all, in the Divine Heart. The negative things we see in history and in ourselves are on the surface of this ocean, and in the depth of it there is peace, there is beauty, there is justice. Yes, if we could realize where we are now we wouldn't have to be concerned with speculating about the nature of Paradise. We would see where we are now. We are either in between Paradise, or hell, or we are in one or the other, or we are on the borderline. We are on the bridge right now, the narrow bridge. I would urge you to continue to inquire and observe where you are now. As frightening as the surface of what you see is, the hatred and all of that, Allah is permitting you to see it. As a child, Allah did not permit you to see it, because you weren't ready to handle it — although there are some children who do see it and know very early what this life is all about at the surface. But don't confuse the surface with the depth. The depth is infinitely meaningful, infinitely beautiful.

Visitor: How far do you let yourself get mixed up in the surface? If you see an injustice being done or something bad being done, how far do you go into that?

Sheikh Nur: All the way. All the way. We are completely committed to humanity and to the human struggle. We are not at all wanting to withdraw anyplace. The thing is that you have to allow yourself to completely participate in the depths too. Because if you just get focused on the surface and start fighting for justice, and you may be supporting some ideological point of view that might help the masses or whatever, then you are definitely going to get trapped into the surface and you won't even be much of a help. You will be part of the problem. Our responsibility is to be in the depths, which is the Divine Attributes. Then, of course, we will act spontaneously. A friend of mine who is a Zen master says that if one of your hands is entering fire the other hand automatically reaches over and pulls it out. It is spontaneous. The other hand doesn't think, "Well, should I risk it? Should I go and get this hand out or not?" That is Tawhid, Unity. When we realize we are one body, one humanity — even closer than one family, we are one body — then there is a spontaneous way of standing up for the rights of others, for justice. This real experience of unity comes from research inside of the Divine Attributes, inside of the Divine Heart. We have to plunge in there. How do you get there? Through prayer and through dhikr, through Divine Remembrance. I hope you can stay for the prayers of the Ramadan which we will make fairly soon. They are extended — we pray 33 raqats, 33 prostrations. There is really a chance to plunge into the ocean there and find pearls or gems.

Is that a satisfactory answer? It is a very important answer because people are always saying, "Oh, you are just interested in religion because you want to escape problems. You are really ignoring the problems of people." It is very important to know that, particularly Islam, among all of the traditions, is totally committed to the struggles of justice. In fact, all of the prophetic traditions are. Let's not diminish any of them. But the modern humanity wants to avoid its religious responsibilities by becoming existentialists: "Oh, isn't the life in the world superficial, isn't it just a jungle of competition?" And then they come up with some ideal like Marxism, for instance, or some other human idea of how to straighten it all out and make it even again, and it becomes worse. Explore the depths of where you are right now.

Visitor: What is an existentialist?

Sheikh Nur: I am just using it in the popular sense. Existentialists are people who say, "I am here now, this is human existence, let's deal with it," but they don't go to any of the revealed books; they don't really make an investigation of what the great human beings have testified to of what human existence is. They end up having a very superficial understanding, usually a negative understanding, even to the point that they feel human existence is ultimately absurd. Then they develop the idea that if you accept the absurdity, that is what gives you your dignity. It is a very tortured way of trying to reach the natural human dignity that we have. We have dignity because Allah gave us this dignity, because we are intimately related to the Being of the Creator, and we have taken a big responsibility directly from the Divine to connect this whole planetary realm. We are really the *khalifatullah*, the representatives of Allah on the planet.

That is what I mean by existentialism, this strange modern illness. But it may not be modern. I am sure there were existentialists of a certain kind around Rasulallah, *Salallahu alayhi wa sallim*. In fact, in Quran it says, *"People are going to come to you and say, 'Are the bones that have turned to dust underneath the desert going to become human form again?'"* An existentialist is saying that: "I can see what human life is — our body turns to dust under the desert and that is it." And Allah informs the Prophet, *"Answer this way..."* In Quran there is nothing that Muhammad, *Salallahu alayhi wa sallim*, himself initiated. He never said, "Well, I will try to give you my answer." The Divine always provided the answers. That is what we mean by well-guided. The Divine answers with a very beautiful analogy: *"When you see a green tree and cut the wood, it turns into a golden fire when you kindle it."* By looking at the green tree could you ever imagine the golden fire? By looking at this physical body, this green tree, could you ever imagine the golden fire of the soul in Paradise?

(Sheikh Nur sings the illahi, *"World has passed away, Allah Allah Lost in Your Embrace..."* The Dervishes join in.)

Sheikh Nur: We have something from our Sheikh Muzaffer which our brother Wali recommended that we read. Read nice and slowly so we can take this in. It is just a couple of pages but it is a very rich and very deep reflection on the tarawih prayer of the Ramadan. It just shows a drop of the vast knowledge of our Sheikh, which is pouring into us at all times. We don't have to feel bereft of knowledge even though we are not book-learned, even though we are unweathered in a scholarly sense. There is knowledge pouring into us.

Dervish Jamal (Reading from Irshad, p. 230-232):

Enlivening the Nights of Ramadan by Performing the Special Tarawih Prayer.

Look at the wages of those who perform these prayers! According to Ali ibn Abi Talib, when our Master was asked about the virtue of the tarawih and the reward for doing them, he said:

"He who does the tarawih on the eve of the first night, becomes as spotlessly clean as when his mother bore him. No trace of sin remains. Except only where the rights of man or beast are concerned! What is due to them must absolutely be discharged.

If you do the tarawih on the second night, Allah will forgive your parents if they died in faith.

If a person does the tarawih on the third night, an angel proclaims from beneath the Throne: 'Your deed was pure!' That is to say, he gives the good news that it has been accepted by Allah, and that your past sins have been pardoned.

He who does the tarawih on the fourth night obtains a reward like that for having read the Holy Quran, the Gospel, the Torah, the Psalms, and the enlightening books.

To him who does the tarawih on the fifth night is given the reward for one who prays at the Sanctuary of the Kaaba, the Prophetic Mosque, and the Mosque called Al-Aqsa.

For one who does the tarawih on the sixth night, the reward is that of having circumambulated the Prosperous House, and rocks and trees seek forgiveness on his behalf.

If you do the tarawih prayers on the seventh night, you are rewarded as if you had aided Moses, on him be peace, in his dispute with Pharaoh and Haman.

The reward for doing the tarawih on the eighth night is that given to Abraham, the special friend of Allah, that is being crowned with the crown of Intimate Friendship.

He who performs the tarawih on the ninth night becomes the beloved of Allah. Allah loves that servant.

He who does the tarawih on the tenth night is endowed with the goodly provisions of this world and the Hereafter.

He who performs the tarawih on the eleventh night will reach his Lord on the day he dies as spotlessly clean as when his mother bore him.

He who does the tarawih on the twelfth night will come to the Place of Resurrection a happy and fortunate person, as radiant as the moon on the fourteenth night.

He who does the tarawih on the thirteenth night will stand secure from fear on the Plain of Arasat.

All the angels witness the prayer of one who does the tarawih on the fourteenth night. That person will escape the reckoning on the Day of Resurrection.

The angels who carry the Throne and Footstool pronounce bene-

dictions on one who performs the tarawih on the fifteenth night.

The fortunate believer who does the tarawih on the sixteenth night receives a document, granting him immunity to the Fire and entitling him to enter Paradise.

One who is present at the tarawih on the seventeenth night receives the reward given to the Prophets, on them be peace.

This reward has been promised to one who performs the tarawih prayers on the eighteenth night: to him an angel will give these good tidings: 'O Abdullah! O beloved servant of Allah! Allah is satisfied with you, your mother and your father!'

To one who performs the tarawih on the nineteenth night, the highest degree of Paradise will be granted.

He who performs the tarawih on the twentieth night will be awarded the rank of the martyrs and the righteous.

A pavilion of light will be made ready in Paradise and presented to him who performs the tarawih on the twenty-first night."

Sheikh Nur: Stop there. That's where we are. Read that one again. We don't want to be abstract. We are talking about the blessings that have been received, so we want to really soak it in. As far as the blessings of the future nights, *Inshallah*, we will consult those night by night. Tonight's blessing —

Dervish Jamal: "A pavilion of light will be made ready in Paradise and presented to him who performs the tarawih on the twenty-first night."

Sheikh Nur: *Al-Fatiha!*

It is a little hard to take in what our brother just read on a very serious level or plane, because, quite frankly, we are really not used to such an exalted level of thinking. Our tendency from our habitual, rational day-to-day level would be to think, "Well, that is beautiful poetry." But that would be a mistake. It would be unfortunate to think of it that way. This way of speaking is much more adequate to reality than the way we ordinarily speak. It is as if we are in front of a spring and we are thirsty and our family is thirsty, but we only have little tiny thimbles to dip the water out with. The bigger the vessel we have, the more water we can dip out, and there is an infinite amount of water here just in these tarawih prayers, for example. The tarawih prayers are like a beautiful spring of healing and life-giving water — not only for us but for all humanity.

We should feel that whatever Allah gives to our hearts flows into the hearts that are joined with ours. It is like an underground cave. If one cave fills up they all fill up to that level, because they are joined underneath. This automatically includes our mother and father, other members of our family, and those of our friends and colleagues who we have been able to make a real heart connection with. It has to be a real connection, obviously. The real dervish lovers attempt to make a heart-connection with all humanity. It is almost an inconceivable feat to even think of trying to do something like this. But they do it because they want every blessing that Allah pours in them to go to all humanity. They become real lovers of humanity. It is not just a pious notion: "O Allah, please benefit all humanity," although, even a pious notion may be accepted by Allah. I am not diminishing anyone's prayer. But the real lovers make a true heart-connection with all humanity. Then they extend it to all of the creations of Allah. A lover of this level is lifting up the whole creation. Let's say that Allah is lifting the whole creation through that person's heart. We aspire in this direction. We know that we have a long way to go, but this is our aspiration. We can certainly begin with our parents. We begin with our mother. She is the most important person to our soul, according to the Rasulallah himself, *Salallahu alayhi wa sallim*. Then we extend out. Someone might say, "Well, my mother is a very impossible person. My mother abandoned me when I was a child," or whatever. All the more reason that one should pray for her and should connect one's heart to her.

Visitor: I am not exactly sure how to explain Islam to my friends who tell me what they read in the papers and are skeptical about it.

Sheikh Nur: I get your point. The point is, Islam cannot be explained. You can't get a sheet of paper with five different points that you can explain to someone that has problems with their perception of Islam. You have to manifest it out of your being. Also, the person has to be ready. If he or she says, "Tell me a little bit about it. I don't like the religion, but maybe you'll tell me something I like," then we don't enter into that kind of discussion. The fact is that in the modern world everything can be explained. You can ask for an answer to everything and we have become obsessed with that. But the depth of something like Islam can only be tasted, can only be experienced directly. You can say one or two things about it, but you say it with the attitude of *Allahu-l-Alim*, Allah is the best Knower. You start that way. If someone asks you something about Islam, you say, "I really don't know, Allah alone really knows these things." The moment you say that the fragrance of Islam comes into the conversation and immediately the person realizes that they are in a different world than they thought they were in. You are not coming with a doctrine, you are coming with an experience.

To be able to in any way enlighten someone about Islam has to be a gift from Allah. We may feel, "Well, I am Muslim from birth, I have read Quran, I have done this or that, I should be able to explain it." But that is not possible, much less ever convert anybody. It is unthinkable to feel that through a series of conversations with someone we can logically move them in a certain direction, and they will eventually embrace Islam. That is an unthinkable type of agenda. Only Allah unveils Muslims in His own unique way and in His own unique time. As you deepen yourself, as you deepen and become a dervish and go deeper and deeper into the spirit of Islam, you will be more and more inspired with things to say. You might speak less, but what you say will have more effect. Thank you for asking the question because I have never really been so clear about the nature of Islam. It is inexpressible. It is not a doctrine. Of course you can always say some clear things, make some clear points about it, but it depends on how you say them. Are you saying them with your lips, with your mind, or are they coming from the depth of your being? Then they will have the desired effect.

Has anyone had dreams? Any questions? (To a dervish) Look at his face. You look beautiful, surrounded by light and joy and contentment. *Alhamdulillah*. And all of you do. This is the holy month, let's not forget that. We are sitting in a Divine Sanctuary. Has anyone had dreams or questions or experiences?

Last night we had a very, very amazing tarawih prayer. I am always asking other people if they have experiences. I should share some of my experiences, the very few that I have. At the end of the twenty raqats we sang the hymn that the people of Medina sang to welcome Rasulallah, *Salallahu alayhi wa sallim,* when he came. So we welcomed and welcomed him. Then we made the three raqats of the witr prayer, and in the third Allahu Akbar — the standing Allahu Akbar, our imam (he told us later) began to silently intercede for all of humanity. Then he began [inwardly] saying, "O Allah show me Your Night of Power, show me Your Night of Power!" At that moment a vast, vast peace opened for him. He said that he never experienced a peace like this before. We all noticed it. We were standing there a little longer than usual, but we didn't feel any anxiety, [as if we should alert him by saying] '*Subhanallah*' or something like that. We were very happy that it was extending. At that time he received a visitation from the Night of Power. The Night of Power, *Inshallah,* will manifest in its fullness on the 27th night according to the richest tradition, but in all of the last ten nights there are visitations from the Night of Power. So he received a real visitation from the Night of Power.

Then we knelt and when I was simply saying, "*As-salamu alayka Ayyuhan Nabiyyu,* peace be upon you, O Noble Prophet," which we always say while kneeling in the prayers, I realized that I was giving my salams to him directly and he was facing me. You don't give your salams to someone's back. You can only give your salams face to face. But it wasn't like a hologram or sort of a psychedelic experience. I didn't see someone in front of me; I just knew he was there and I was giving my salams to him. It was a tremendously powerful experience and I began weeping. Ahmed Halil was next to me and he knew exactly what I was experiencing, because tears are the primary sign of seeing Rasulallah, *Salallahu alayhi wa sallim,* and having an immediate contact with him. There is no way that you won't shed tears either outwardly or inwardly at that time. In fact, it is an important sign that it is not imagination. We tend to think, "Well, maybe I imagined that."

After the prayers, one of our sisters, Batul, said that at that very same time, during those last three raqats, she felt this vast mist descending over the entire congregation. It was like a cloud, a radiant cloud, and she was saying inside of herself, "It is Rasulallah, it is Rasulallah." This happened just last night on the twentieth night of our prayers. We have been having wonderful prayers all the way along, but we never reached this level. This was the inauguration of the last ten days of Ramadan, which is an entirely different, new level in the Ramadan. I am praying and hoping and I feel that tonight, on the twenty-first, which is the first odd numbered night in the last ten days, (a very, very powerful and important night, the night of the passing away of Hazreti Ali, may his countenance be ennobled and enlightened), *Inshallah,* we will have these kind of experiences. I want you all to be extremely alert to this. Not that we should force anything or project anything. I had no idea; I was just doing the prayer in the most simple manner ...*As-salam alayka Ayyuhan Nabiyyu*... exactly the same thing I have said hundreds of times, and he was there, I knew it. Wait for that kind of thing, and if you don't have that type of experience don't feel that you have missed out, either.

In Efendi's meditation on the tarawih prayers, it says that for the people who make the prayers tonight, a pavilion of Light is being prepared for them in Paradise, and that pavilion of Light can be experienced here. It is not something that is on the other side of a wall or something. Paradise is not in space, not in time. He doesn't say, "For the people who see a pavilion of Light, then a pavilion of Light is being prepared." It is for everyone who prays on the twenty-first night. Please feel that this is the night of the pavilion of Light for all of us. We should have the inner spiritual confidence and certainty about that, whatever that ultimately might mean. We are not trying to define it or limit it. A pavilion of Light: it is an opening. A pavilion is something that does not have walls. It is a pavilion, yet it is open to the landscape, it is open to infinity. This is the promise for all of us tonight. Simply having that confidence we don't feel we have to say, "O Allah, show me a flash of light," or something like that. This is possibly a petty way of thinking. If Allah shows us something we say, *Alhamdulillah*. We accept it and we are moved by it, but we are not pestering, saying, "O Lord, show me this, show me that." He did show us — we read from the Efendi's book tonight. We have been shown what this night is, so with all sincerity we should go and offer our prayer in that totally open spirit.

Everyone here can be confirmed that they are part of a full participation of this night. We don't make any borders and boundaries between initiates and non-initiates here. The people here are human beings, and as such are *khalifatullah*, the representative of Allah on this planet. I welcome you all here, I congratulate you on reaching the twenty-first night, and I wish you great realization in the prayers of this night together.

Al-Fatiha... Amin. Ya Allah Hu.

Lex Hixon received his Ph.D. in World Religions from Columbia University in 1976. From about 1971 to the late 80's he conducted a weekly radio show in New York City called "In The Spirit," interviewing spiritual teachers from around the world. Among his books are *Great Swan, Mother of the Universe, Heart of the Koran, Atom from the Sun of Knowledge, Mother of the Buddhas,* and *Living Buddha Zen.* For more information inquire at: **www.lexhixon.org** For "In The Spirit" Series information inquire at: **www.srv.org**

◆ *John Francis*

The Jesus Way of Meditation
Biblical Insights in Universal Light

Today's churches have forgotten that Jesus taught meditation. He did so to help us fulfill the "greatest commandment," to love God totally and neighbors as oneself. It was an inner, heart-centered discipline conveyed via enigmatic sayings and parables, and the method involved relaxing, stilling, and purifying the physical, emotional, and mental levels to awaken the feeling and expression of Divine Love. The ultimate intention for this was to fulfill the divine purpose for incarnation on Earth — the cultivation of God individualized. The secrecy surrounding His parables is consistent with inner teachings only suitable for the spiritually mature, psychologically stable, and morally upright.

Jesus, in effect, taught what Saint John of the Cross called "the science of Love." Similarities can also be found in the Christian Hesychast psycho-physiological practices for bringing the head-mind down into the sacred heart in the center of the soul.

In exploring this Jesus way we will begin with its intention and then consider the method. This is because intention is far more important than method. Different or no methods with the same intention can lead to the same outcome.

The "Lord's Prayer" may have been said immediately before meditation to clearly invoke and firmly establish an intention: *"Our Father who art in heaven, hallowed be Thy name, Thy Kingdom come, Thy will be done on Earth as it is in heaven …"*

The Prodigal Soul

Jesus told a parable about a father who had two sons. There was a prodigal son who went wandering off to the "far country" and squandered his inheritance on "riotous living." After becoming totally destitute he turned around and headed back to his father's house. Seeing the returning son from afar, the father ran to greet him. Overjoyed, the father held a big celebration, put his finest robe on his returning son, and placed a ring on his finger.

The other son never wandered and was very resentful of the special treatment his brother received. He complained that even though he obeyed all his father's rules, he was never given such gifts.

Like all the Jesus parables this one is highly symbolic. It goes to the heart of the human condition. Both sons were seeking fulfillment. The prodigal son first looked outward to the "far country," the outer world of sensual indulgence, for his fulfillment. It was only after suffering that he "came to his senses" and returned to his Father's house in the Kingdom of God and there found fulfillment. The other son never found total satisfaction by merely obeying the external rules of moral behavior and remained bitter and jealous.

This parable addresses both the cause of human suffering and the purpose of our experience on Earth. Suffering results from seeking fulfillment in the temporary, unreliable outer world. That is why Jesus said: *"Seek first the Kingdom of God and all things shall be added unto you"* and *"the Kingdom of God is within."* It is not found by merely adhering to outward rules, but by turning attention inward to the Source of all life. In the parable we also see that old adage: *"When we take one step inward toward God, God takes a thousand steps outward toward us."*

Constricted by fear and distracted by desires, we live continually deprived of feeling Divine Love. Instead we feel empty and restless, from which Love's imitations provide no lasting relief. Saint Augustine wisely observed: *"Our hearts are restless until they rest in Thee."* Yet, since we originate in Love, the purpose of incarnating on Earth cannot be to find Love. We are deprived of feeling Universal Love and its power by cosmic design as motivation to cultivate the inner seed of Love, and thus become God individualized.

In the prodigal soul parable, the returning son is clothed in the "best" robe. This robe metaphorically refers to Divine Radiance. It is not a covering, but a direct emanation from the Divine center point of the soul.

It is only when sufficient Radiance has been cultivated that one can be permanently liberated from the human condition of suffering. That is why, in the wedding feast parable, an invited guest who shows up without the proper *"wedding garment"* (Divine Radiance) is cast into the *"outer darkness"* of the *"weeping and gnashing of teeth"* (Matthew 22:13). Conversely, those with white *"robes"* have triumphantly overcome the world (Revelation 7:14).

Jesus could have told a parable where a son returns to his previous status, but instead He wants to convey that we are radically enlightened and empowered (the ring metaphor) as an individualized aspect of God by "leaving" undifferentiated consciousness, plunging into matter, and then awakening from the "dream" of human existence. There is a higher purpose to living on Earth beyond just having a human experience. Carl Jung, the renowned mystic psychiatrist, called it *"individuation."*

Cultivating the Center Point

Jesus taught meditation consistent with the original root-meaning of the word — meditari — "being returned to the center." The root, "med," occurs in median, medium, Mediterranean and even medicine. Apparently, at one time, medicine was considered a way to restore health through harmony with an inner center.

There is an ancient saying: *"God is a circle with a center everywhere and a circumference nowhere."* The renowned Rabbi, Maimonides, also referred to the *"wondrous central point."* It is upon this still, omnipresent center that we focus our inner attention in the original meaning of meditation.

We can thus live centered, and move calmly amidst turmoil, in the *"peace that passes all understanding."* In stillness is found the "mustard seed" of Divine potential, the point from which the individual emerges from the infinite, formless God. It is the point of life on Earth (note how we use "point" synonymously with "meaning," and to have no meaning is to be "pointless.").

Jesus likened the Kingdom of God to a *"mustard seed"* that can grow into a large tree. However, few cultivate that seed. Therefore, *"The harvest is great but the laborers few,"* and, *"Lift up your eyes and look on the fields, for they are white already to harvest"* (John 4:35).

The Chandogya Upanishad (3:14:3) uses the metaphor of the mustard seed for the Atman (Divine Self) located deep within the spiritual heart, accessible in every human through an inner gateway (*chakra*) in the center of the chest.

The purpose of the Jesus meditation is to facilitate the unfoldment of the divine human potential latent in everyone from birth. It is a way of cultivating that "mustard seed" so that it grows to be great. In doing so, we realize ourselves as "sons (and daughters) of God," or more descriptively, as radiant suns of God. Meister Eckhart, the Christian mystic, said: *"Pear seeds grow into pear trees, and God seeds grow into God."* Also, Saint Athanasius boldly proclaimed: *"For the Son of God became man so that we might become God."*

Thus, Jesus offers an answer to the age-old question, what is the purpose of being born on Earth and why is there so much suffering? *"Unless a grain of wheat falls into the ground and dies, it abides alone: but if it dies, it brings forth much fruit"* (John 12:24). Here, Jesus uses "die" as a metaphor for a temporary loss of spiritual awareness. Similarly, Jesus said the prodigal son was "dead" before returning to his father's house.

So, Jesus seems to be saying that the spiritual "death" that occurs when an individual Self incarnates on Earth is necessary for the spiritual growth of the inner-divine seed. Furthermore, if God did not project into material creation as "seeds," God would remain "alone" as one-undifferentiated Self.

The trials and tribulations of incarnation form the "soil" within which the divine seed grows. It provides the motivation to cultivate the radiance of the divine center point in each of us.

Another Jesus metaphor is the *"pearl of great price."* A pearl starts as a grain of sand that grows in beauty in response to irritation.

It is an enlightened body that Jesus spoke of when He said, *"If thine eye be single thy whole body shall be full of light."* (Matthew 6:22). In the meditation of Jesus that "single eye" is contacted in the cave of the spiritual heart and its illumination felt as radiant Love. This is also referred to by Meister Eckhart: *"The eye with which I see God is the very same eye by which God sees me."*

Inner radiance is sometimes experienced first as a "star" before appearing as an all-purifying, blazing Sun of God. Thus, the "birth" of Christ in the "manger" of the heart is metaphorically heralded by the "Star of Bethlehem." *"And take heed ..... until the day dawns and the day star rises in your hearts."* (II Peter 1:19). Saint Therese wrote of the "star of love." Saint Symeon, the New Theologian, described an inner experience of a *"star that nourishes and heals"* and expands. Most importantly, Jesus says in the Book of Revelation 22:16: I am *"the bright and morning star."*

The Endless Unfoldment

Many meditation teachings in the East contend that the ultimate goal is extrication from the illusions of embodied life and permanent dissolution in formlessness. One school says the formless state is an utterly empty void, while another says it is actually a plenum — infinitely full. This later view says that the One God becomes many individual selves for the play, and that the goal of the individual is to merge back and dissolve in the infinite, formless One. The voidists, however, entirely deny the reality of God or a Self.

The intentions and beliefs underlying a meditation practice can have serious, long-term consequences. For example, the Tibetan, Lama Lodo, has written in *"Quintessence of the Animate and Inanimate"* that those who meditate upon an imagined, empty void may eventually get themselves stuck in just such a mental creation upon physical death. Lama Lodo also writes that Lord Buddha may have to compassionately come and extricate these meditators from their self-created entrapment.

Fully remembering our immortal Self does eradicate the root of suffering. But after that realization, is God's play finished in and through that individual Self? Jesus and cer-

ADVAITA-SATYA-AMRITAM 39

tain spiritual masters say no. There is a Divine Life whereby an enlightened individual, *Jivatman/Jivanmukti*, continues expression but without the illusion of separation from the One, Universal Consciousness. How is that possible?

According to Vedanta, the sense of ego-separateness results from the individual's false self-identification with the three bodies (biological, emotional/mental, causal) and five sheaths within that triad that encase the individualized, incarnated Self. The false ego thinks and feels like: "I am this finite, mortal body."

However, an individual existence not based on a personality composite of the three bodies and five sheaths is possible. Consider an individual Self expressing as a self-emanating radiant point-source of consciousness that is not covered by veils of separative illusions. Actually, every human has a radiant-point source (Atman) in the central-spiritual heart waiting to be cultivated. This radiance can be felt, seen, heard, or even smelled and tasted.

When Jesus said, *"Men do not light a candle and put it under a bushel, but on a candlestick,"* He called forth our inner Radiance. Saint Teresa of Avila discovered increasingly *"interior castles"* that hide this Light.

Some refer to our inner Radiance as a "light body," but it is not a body in the sense of a container. Rather, it is an individualized emanation from the Sun of God. It can also be likened to a wave that rises up from the ocean. In the Indian Vaishnava tradition, this spiritual "body" is called *"Siddha-Deha,"* and manifests through total devotion, purification, and surrender to God.

Jesus said, when speaking from oneness with God: *"I am the vine and you are the branches."* A branch is an outgrowth of a vine and not something that covers it. He also said to *"love your neighbor as yourself,"* which is consistent with the view of one Self shining through all. Thus, Jesus could declare that when you act charitably toward a needy person you are actually doing so to Jesus Himself. Vedanta explicitly states that there is ultimately only one Self living and unfolding through the many life forms. So this is perhaps why Saint Catherine could say, after an ecstatic experience: "My *me is God."*

The Way of the Parables

Having thoroughly considered meditation intention, let us now look at the method Jesus imparted via His mysterious sayings and parables. Space here does not permit a detailed discussion. That will be offered in a forthcoming book. Also, there will be no attempt in the following to give specific meditation instruction. That is always best done in a direct teacher-student relationship where both are spiritually mature, morally upright, and psychologically stable.

Jesus often counseled against worry, hardening of the heart, and having a "stiff neck," because these interfere with the inflow of Divine Grace. It is also helpful to conserve life-force energy to interiorize attention in meditation. For this we can look to the parables regarding the wise and foolish use of the five senses (*"bridesmaids,"* Matthew 25:1-12) and *"girding one's loins"* (Luke 12:35) to get teachings for the redirection of procreative energy up into the heart-center during meditation.

Jesus taught to begin meditation at the physical and move inward to more subtle levels, surrendering along the way to the radiant Divine Love emanating from the center. Thus, Jesus advises that when sitting at the "feast" start with the lowest seat (or room; Luke 14:7-12). Also, there is the parable (Matthew 20:16) of hiring sequentially five groups of laborers representing moving from outer to inner through the five sheaths (koshas) that surround the central radiance of the soul. Laborers getting "paid" in the reverse order of "hiring" is symbolic of the central radiance moving from inner to outer. The same amount of pay signifies the same Grace being imparted.

The parable (Luke 15:8) of sweeping a house in search of a tenth and "lost coin" is actually a search for the center point of the soul. The Zen saying, *"breath sweeps the mind,"* is applicable here. The other nine coins refer to the nine openings of the senses, procreation, and elimination.

To facilitate receptivity to inner radiance, Jesus taught *"mixing leaven in three measures of dough until the whole was leavened"* (Matthew 13:33). Metaphorically, this is intentionally absorbing prana (soul energy) into the physical, emotional, and mental levels to increase permeability and responsiveness to the inner Sun of God. This is facilitated by intention, and by continual, disengaged, and total feeling of respiration during meditation.

Finally, the unfolding of the Kingdom of God in the human body is described metaphorically by Jesus as a grain seed that grows *"first the stem, then the head, then the mature grain in the head"* (Mark 4:28). This is a reference to the movement of the Divine Fire up the spinal column (*sushumna*), *"the straight and narrow way"* through the spiritual heart-center into the brain stem, and then into the cranial region (*sahasrara*). This completes "theosis" — the resurrection and divinization of the human person.

John Francis is a retired college professor who lives as a lay-Christian, contemplative monk. Communication is welcomed: johnf153@hotmail.com.

Michael S. Isaacs

OVERCOMING OBSTACLES TO
Sitting Meditation

Many attempt sitting meditation but few stay on the path. This article will apply to all forms of sitting meditation focusing on a particular object, whether the goal is relaxation, stress-reduction, or spiritual growth. The content reflects the personal experience I have had over many years as a psychotherapist, practitioner, and teacher of body-mind modalities, and spiritual seeker. The ideas and strategies in this article hopefully will be of value to those considering meditation, beginners, and students practicing meditation for many years.

Why is the dropout rate so high in meditation? First, it is not easy to introduce, get started, and stay with any new path. Any change for good is difficult. We fear change, do not want to let go of bad habits. So while most know the importance of proper diet and exercise, how difficult it is to take the steps required to accomplish these ends! Busy schedules, conflicting priorities, and psychological blocks can get in the way and become excuses to do what needs to be done. If changing habits were easy, would we need so many New Year's resolutions? For those interested in how to stay motivated in order to effect desired change, I refer you to my article "How to Develop a Daily Relaxation Practice" on my website, michaelisaacs.net

Second, meditation is basically alien to the Western mind. Our society is oriented towards materialism and competition. Much good can come from this involvement. Nevertheless, these strivings are focused on the external rather than the internal world. In contrast, in Oriental cultures it is more natural to go within for happiness. In these societies, meditation has been around for thousands of years.

Third, in the meditation process itself, the most challenging obstacle is discouragement over not being able to sufficiently control the wandering mind. As a former yoga teacher, I heard over and over again these themes from meditation drop-outs: "I just can't control my mind"; "I can't do this – the mind distractions drive me crazy," "I'm not succeeding so why bother"; "focusing on my mantra is impossible"; and "I wanted more peace, but in meditation my thoughts, feelings, and racing mind have become worse." No one likes to fail, to feel not good enough, not worthy, and not successful.

Controlling the mind is no easy task. This was known thousands of years ago by the sages in India. Here are some pertinent passages from the Bhagavad Gita. When the word "mind" is used, the sages meant mind and emotions, thoughts and feelings.

"Doubtless …the mind is restless and hard to control; but by practice and detachment, it can be restrained."

"For the mind is restless, turbulent, powerful, and obstinate. To control it is as hard as to control the wind."

In the late 1800's and early 1900's, Swami Vivekananda, one of the first illumined souls from India to visit the United States, wrote: *"How hard it is to control the mind. Well has it been compared to a maddened monkey!"*

In this article I will at times use the letters DTF for a distracting thought and feeling. And when I write about mind it includes both mind and feelings. The first part of this article will show how to deal with the obstacles of mind distractions. The second part will explain how they are not just nuisances, but how they actually make valuable contributions to the meditation experience.

Don't Battle DTFs

As a tool, we must realize that, except for rare individuals, staying completely focused on an object of meditation without multiple mind distractions is impossible. The secret is to give up the battle to eliminate mind interference. Never expect to willfully defeat them. When you recognize that they are diverting you from your object of meditation, without judgment and self-blame, return to the object.

As we proceed, we can next understand meditation as firstly focusing on an object of meditation, secondly recognizing one or more DTFs, and lastly returning to the object. This repetitive cycle is the "practice" of meditation. Thus, the practice of meditation calls for adapting, tolerating, and coexisting with the distracted mind. There is an ancient Yogic observation: *"Being free from thoughts does not mean stopping thoughts."* And, an old Chinese proverb: *"You may not be able to avoid birds flying above your head, but you can prevent them from building nests in your hair."*

Types of DTFs

It is helpful to understand the nature of various intervening mind distractions. By understanding their patterns over a period of time, you will be able to recognize and dismiss them sooner when they surface. We can often anticipate the nature of these distractions immediately prior to sitting. For example, if you had a heated argument with your partner before the meditation, it is likely that some aspect of this incident will arise as a distraction. Awareness of the nature of your mind interferences may be realized during the meditation period or after your meditation when you have had time to review them over in your mind.

Thought DTFs

Thought distractions are predominantly about thoughts as differentiated from those that are predominantly about feelings. The following hypothetical situation involves a thought. A stockbroker works in a large city and commutes to and from the suburbs. He usually drives to work, but occasionally, if the weather is bad, he travels by train. One morning when he arises, he looks out the window and observes rainy weather. Thereafter, during his usual morning meditation, he has a distracting thought about whether or not he should take the car or the train. The effect as he experienced it was a simple thought, without any accompanying emotion.

Here are other thoughts some of which could further be labeled in one's mind as trivial or humorous: "What will I have for dinner?" "I think I forgot to turn off the computer." "I wonder if ten minutes are up." "What am I doing here?" "I wonder what day it is." "I can't remember what I had for breakfast?"

Feeling DTFs

Feeling distractions are predominantly about emotions. They are heart centered, energized, or charged, and sometimes passionate. They can be positive or negative. Positive feelings are pleasant and exciting. Examples are sense pleasures such as enjoyment of nature, food, and love. Other positive feeling DTFs are the passion and joy of creative and inspired ideas.

Negative feelings can be disturbing and intense. Examples of negative effects are fear, guilt, envy, worry, jealousy, anger, and lust. The emergence of these feelings can be jarring. Practitioners often think that meditation will lead them to peace, but in the quiet of meditation often comes disharmony, turbulence, and discord! Later I will explain how these emotional experiences can be of great value.

Body DTFs

Certain mind distractions can be attributed to such bodily disturbances as pain, noise, and other sensations. Most of us will experience body sensations in meditation such as itching, coughing, sneezing, yawning, and a running nose. To one who is committed to regular meditation, these pose no problem.

Pain in the body can range from heavy duty pain to slight pain. If the pain is great, then common sense would be to put off the meditation to another time when the pain ceases or is sufficiently lessened. If the pain is tolerable, try to treat both the pain itself and the feelings about the pain in the usual way as described in this article.

Noise as a disruption often poses a major obstacle to beginning students of meditation, because they are not familiar with the quietness of going inward. Noise can be fatal to aspiring beginners. Therefore, for beginners, it is particularly important to meditate in a quiet atmosphere. It has been said that experienced aspirants would not be distracted doing meditation sitting in a boiler room or sitting on the steps of the library in a big city.

Labeling

A term for designating and classifying DTFs is labeling. In labeling, one part of the mind witnesses, observes, and categorizes the other part of the mind that is diverting one away from the meditation object. One way to label and dismiss a DTF is to view it according to the different types mentioned above — that is, thought, feeling, or body. If the distraction is a thought such as "I wonder what I had for breakfast," one might label it "trivial thought." If it is "What am I doing here in meditation," one

might label it "only an excuse thought."

If the distraction is a positive feeling such as "My wife will enjoy the roses I have bought for her, and I am looking forward to surprising her tonight," one could label it "delay feeling." If the interference is a negative feeling, such as "That idiot irked me," one could label it "annoyance feeling." If the distraction is about body concern such as "I wish this coughing would stop," you might label it "body, not now."

Another way to label and dismiss a DTF is to frame it in terms of present, past, or future experiences. Like dreams, they are often stimulated by events that happened twenty-four hours prior or after the meditation. A mind interruption about an experience in the present moment is body pain. This may distract you not only because of the pain itself, but for mental effects such as annoyance and fear. Upon recognition of this distraction you might say to yourself "Not now."

Here are two hypothetical situations about experiences from the past. One situation involved a reaction by a person watching a TV mystery film in the evening. The film was packed with action. It made a significant impression on the viewer. In the morning meditation, he found that he was flooded with DTFs about the stimulating film.

Another situation involved a verbal dispute in the early evening between husband and wife. Wife was upset with negative feelings of hurt and anger. In her meditation soon after the fracas she had many turbulent mental interruptions about this incident.

Both of the above mind interferences involved feelings about experiences from the immediate past. Upon recognition of the distractions in both cases, self talk to help one return to the meditation object might be labeled, "Choose now."

An example of a DTF about an incident in the future was

precipitated in the morning when a woman and her partner agreed to talk after dinner about important financial matters. In her usual late afternoon meditation the partner found it difficult to meditate due to the flooding of ideas about what to say at the meeting. Upon recognition of this challenge the helpful label could be, "See you later."

After meditating for many years I observed a pattern that many of my mind disturbances stemmed from my immediate past. Since I am a conscientious and earnest psychotherapist, after a session, DTFs frequently arise evaluating how the session went. If I have a moment after the session for a brief meditation, these interruptions will often appear on the scene. Since I have become aware of performance distractions, I am more quickly able to recognize, label, and dismiss them. I might say to myself something like "Here I go again performance; forget it for now."

However, a more frequent pattern of mine are DTFs about the immediate future. These are anticipations of both pleasant and worrisome activities coming up. Such a worrisome mind distraction arose during meditation recently. My mind drifted to worry about an airplane flight from San Francisco to New York. Two days ago my brother and sister-in-law's flight had been cancelled due to lightning storms. They were leaving that afternoon and I was hoping that their flight would have no further delays.

Since future oriented mind ramblings plague me the most, I try to remember to deflect them quickly when I have a hunch immediately before a meditation time that they will emerge during the meditation.

DTF Strategies Prior to and During Meditation

The more active the mind has been prior to meditating, the more chances are that one will be flooded with DTFs. Therefore, if possible, one should move into a relaxation mode before sitting. This allows sufficient time to distance from moments of stressful thinking and emotions. For some, this may mean meditation early in the morning, having rested from a night's sleep, and before the household awakens. For others, it may mean after a day's work, when the surge of work effort has calmed down. Another auspicious time might be in the evening when the day's activities have subsided.

Another strategy is to sit in the quiet for a designated time just to let the mind think or feel whatever it wants to. This type of meditation, which I call witness meditation, can be an effective way to lessen the challenges of mind interference. In this paradigm there is no specific object of meditation other than to observe the movements of the mind. One might simply sit and watch thoughts and feelings as they pass through the blank screen of the mind's inner vision. As an observer, you are not seeing them as distractions or impediments, but as appearances. As such, there is less pressure to allow them to drag you into their drama. You are in a position to even welcome and look forward to observe what will next appear. You might call them WTFs, standing for "witness or welcomed thoughts and feelings!"

If you are comfortable with imagery, consider an analogy that mind appearances in witness meditation are analogous to clouds or ships. Visualize that you are sitting on a beach at the ocean. In meditation, you are looking straight ahead witnessing clouds or ships as WTFs moving in a straight line horizontally across your mind screen. Imagine the thoughts or feelings as clouds or ships appearing in front of you until they disappear out of sight, or until another cloud or ship comes into view. This type of meditation can reduce the conflict one faces in traditional sitting meditation between object and DTFs. This is because, in witness meditation, observing the manifestations of mind is one's sole object. WTFs are the only entity to focus on. One's only involvements are the WTFs passing by and the moments of silence that may appear in between their coming and going.

Another way to segue into a more relaxed state before the actual meditation is to practice brief mind modalities such as deep breathing, imagery, stretching, chanting, and qigong. Since deep breathing is one of the quickest ways to achieve relaxation, one may also want to practice deep breathing techniques. One may find all or parts of this centering exercise helpful as a preliminary step for grounding prior to meditation, because it includes so many calming down techniques — breathing, imagery, soothing self talk, and involvement in the present moment.

Such pre-meditation techniques can include aids such as: Take a few moments to be present. Let your eyes gently close. Take a deep relaxing breath and breathe in calm energy. Breathe out tension, fatigue, and worry. With each breath become more and more present. Any thoughts or feelings that flow through your mind, just notice them and let them go. Any issues that need further thought, merely choose to put them away and come back to them later. Let your mind, body, and spirit be peaceful and in harmony.

Included in this exercise are four important suggestions in dealing with DTFs. That is: notice them as soon as possible; let them go; deal with certain ones at a future time; make a conscious choice to stay in the present moment. These choices empower one to attain a measure of dominion over the "monkey mind."

Prior to starting the meditation object focus, and even as reminders during the meditation, use these powerful lines from the centering exercise to generally set the framework for dealing with mind obstacles: any thoughts or feelings that flow through my mind, I notice and let them go; any issues that need further thought I choose to put them away and come back to them later. One may also want to utilize any of one's favorite affirmations, denials, self talk, and truth-statements once one realizes the mind's involvement with a DTF, such as "This is my time"; "I permit myself to take this time to go inward"; and, "I allow myself this period to be free of usual mind distractions."

Some brief self statements upon recognition of mind interference are as follows: Move back; Let go; Pass by; Go away; Not now; Back to the present; Go back; Bye for now; See you later; Bye-bye; Pass away; Back to the center; Oh well; Stop thinking; Stop it; and Enough.

Most people who meditate say the above statements gently. However, this does not preclude saying them in a forceful tone, which may work for those who have assertive personalities. In this case, exerting some force is not to battle DTFs, but to coexist with them more effectively. These assertions can be used in waking or active meditation as well. Swami Vivekananda had an experience with aggressive baboons in the mountains when he was young, and when he started to run from them he heard a voice saying, "Face the brutes!" He used this command in meditation to teach others not to run away from challenges.

The final strategy I would offer is to use breathing techniques to calm down the mind so one can reduce the chaos and return to normal focusing. Among these techniques are focusing attention to the breathing if the breath is not your meditation object, increasing the duration of time on both the inhale and exhale, and alternate nostril yoga breathing.

Benefits of DTFs

When writing about benefits of mind interference, I am not suggesting that we meditate with the primary reason of reaping their benefits. The primary goal in meditation is focusing on the object of meditation as much as possible. I am merely cautioning to avoid becoming distracted or put off when they frequently appear. Appreciating the positive aspects of mind distractions will help one avoid discouragement.

Key benefits of DTFs are emptying the mind of clutter, inducing moments of silence, and releasing charged ideas and emotions from the unconscious mind.

Emptying the Mind

Here are a few quotes from diverse and well-known persons who have undertaken the meditation process. The famous writer, Deepak Chopra, M.D., and adherent of transcendental meditation, stated: *"Meditation is not a way of making the mind quiet, but rather a way of entering into the quiet that's already there, buried under the fifty thousand thoughts an average person thinks a day."* The Japanese Zen meditation author, Katsuki Sekida, has written: *"In this stillness...emptiness...the source of all kinds of activity is latent. It is the state that we call pure existence."* Albert Einstein wrote, *"Out of clutter, find simplicity."* The Chinese master Wu-Men wrote: *"Ten thousand flowers in spring, the moon in autumn, the cool breeze in summer, snow in winter. If your mind isn't clouded by unnecessary things, this is the best season of your life."*

No matter whether DTFs are thoughts, feelings, or body distractions, they have the effect of emptying the mind of clutter — and this is good. Another similar construct to emptying the mind and allowing mind space is opening the mind.

The number of thoughts that we carry around all day is staggering. Many of these thoughts are repetitive, and therefore energy draining. Henry Grayson, Ph.D, a psychoanalyst-metaphysician has calculated that most of us have approximately 72,000 thoughts daily. With this volume of thoughts a day, can we not wonder why so many DTFs invade our space when we try to meditate?

Visualize a person going on a train carrying a heavy piece of luggage. He stands in the aisle holding the luggage. He doesn't realize that he can put the luggage up in a compartment or drop the luggage on to the floor. Taking this step relieves him of a heavy weight. The quiet of meditation affords the opportunity to empty the mind of some of its baggage effect. Not only can DTFs free the mind from conscious and unconscious clutter during the day, they can reduce thoughts and feelings that prevent one up from sleeping, and from spiritual experiences.

Personal Insights

One morning in the past I had an epiphany where I appreciated how emptying the mind benefited me. I had set my goal to sit twenty minutes. For almost the entire time I was entangled with various mind effects. I was basically digesting and summarizing in my mind the events that included what happened the day before at work, a dream I had the night before, and other trivia. At the last minute or so of my allotted time, I realized that I had spent only a very small time focusing on my meditation object. Finally, in the remaining time, I was able to focus on point.

I was disappointed with myself for this lack of concentration. However, for the rest of my day, when I did my "mini-meditations," there was little mind chatter and my meditation focus was much improved. Then I realized that I had accomplished something simply by the emptying of clutter of the DTFs in the morning. There was a need, apparently, for me to do this emptying process. This clearing paved the way for more focused mini-meditations during the day, and for bringing general clarity to my mind. I became thankful that my distractions in the morning meditation had substantially emptied my mind for the upcoming day.

How emptying the mind can be an attribute for inspired thoughts is illustrated by the work of the inventor Thomas Edison. His hearing was greatly impaired. In the latter part of his life he was asked how he accomplished so much in his life. He replied that among the reasons was his hardness of hearing. It enabled him to avoid much of the advice, suggestions, and chatter from the world. It has been said that in his room he was often seen with his hand cupped over his ears. It seemed that he was listening to the universe for creative ideas, which resulted in his great scientific discoveries.

With his hearing problem, Edison was able to reduce or possibly eliminate mind influences in leisure time and during work. Because his mind was basically empty of clutter, he had more space and mental energy to imbibe inspired thought. Making an analogy to meditation we can say that his mind space allowed him to focus more clearly on his "meditation object," which was silence that afforded creativity. This brings me to the next topic which is the relationship between mind distraction and silence.

The Silent Moment

Silent moments are times of non-thinking, beyond words and thoughts. There is an Arabian proverb which runs, *"The fruit of silence is tranquility."* Ralph Waldo Emerson commented: *"I like the silent church before the service begins better than any preacher."* Elizabeth Kubler-Ross wrote: *"Learn to get in touch with the silence within."*

The quiet moment appears between the time when the DTF is acknowledged and the time when the practitioner returns his

> "While Freud emphasized the pathogenic sexual and aggressive aspects of the human psyche, psychoanalyst Carl Jung added an appreciation of artistic and creative importations coming from the depths of the unconscious. Jung was interested in life energizing "visions" coming out of the unconscious."

focus back to the meditation object. This imperceptible silent moment brings that instant of inner peace and rest. It is akin to nature's wisdom in the process of breathing, and the heart functioning. In breathing, nature provides a slight pause [Kumbhaka] before and after every inhalation and after every exhalation. Similarly, with each heartbeat there is a brief pause before and after each heartbeat.

The Hindu Yogis achieve spiritual enlightenment when the much repeated Sanskrit mantra word or phrase disappears into the silence. Hence there is the term "lighten" in the word enlightenment. For those not meditating purely for spiritual goals, the silent moments can abet intuition, artistic ideas, and moments of peace.

Let us imagine that we have 100% concentration on the meditation object such as the breath, and therefore there are no distractions. Wouldn't this deprive us of the benefits of silent moments between the interplay of object and DTFs? Without the interplay between mind interference and the return to meditation object focus, the silent moment could not take place.

Often, suspending concentration on an object is a good thing. Suppose we lose our keys. We frantically try to locate them. We have no success. How often, when we forget about the search, lo and behold, we discover the keys without trying to find them! In other words, we solved the problem by moving away from focusing on the problem. We know that many artists produce their best work when they are not thinking about their art. Many writers carry around a pad to write down ideas that come to them when their minds are resting from their work involvement. You are probably familiar with the expression "When you least expect it, the bride cometh."

The benefit of empty space is illustrated in Fire a poem by Judy Sorum Brown:

What makes a fire burn
 Is space between logs
 A breathing space....
 The space is there,
 With openings
 In which the flame
 That knows just how it wants to burn
 Can find its way

Release of Negative and Positive Emotions

Negative and positive charged DTFs can bring benefits in a way similar to that which can be achieved in psychoanalysis and psychoanalytic psychotherapy. I can not emphasize enough that it is negative emotions that play a large role in discouraging people to stay with their meditation. By using the term "negative," it should not be construed that negative emotions are bad. Emotions are negative only in the sense that they are by nature upsetting. But keeping them buried is not mentally healthy.

Parental and societal environments have so often crushed our spirits by not allowing us to be "sad, mad, and glad." Joan Borysenko, PhD, the author of Minding the Body, Mending the Mind, writes: "It's hiding feelings, believing that you have no right to experience them, and therefore feeling helpless that can lead us to a more dangerous state...." "...The only negative emotions are emotions that you will not allow yourself or someone else to experience. Negative emotions will not harm you if you express them appropriately and then let them go...." "...bottling them up is far worse...." "...love and laughter are key attitudes for healing, but they can only be experienced after we let go of the negative attitudes that block their expression."

In my article, "Psychotherapy and Spirituality," I echoed the ideas of Borysenko and others that the inability to appreciate, communicate, understand, and gain access to feelings has caused an incalculable amount of suffering in the world. Sigmund Freud, the founder of psychoanalysis and the father of all psychotherapy practices that emerged thereafter, discovered the importance of unearthing hidden thoughts and feelings to alleviate mental and physical discord. He tapped into the pathological aspects of the unconscious, particularly aggressive and sexual instincts which he labeled as the "id." Psychoanalysis was a methodology where the unconscious could gradually become conscious, giving us the opportunity for analysis and self growth.

Contributions of Freud and Jung

Two of Freud's methods of treatment were free association and the interpretation of dreams. In free association one is encouraged to let the mind drift to whatever comes up without censoring the material. This allows repressed unconscious material to emerge. Negative charged emotions can therefore move from the unconscious to the conscious so we can become aware of them and understand them. Similarly, in the silence of meditation, negative charged DTFs are the equivalent of unconscious manifestations of free association.

Dreams are another avenue where negative emotions are released. Most of my recall around dreams, like most of my patients, seem to revolve around negative charged emotions such as anxiety and fear. This is no accident since these effects, being troublesome, are the most likely to be repressed, and therefore the most in need of emerging into the light of consciousness for bringing about mental health.

In the psychoanalytic study of dreams there is a theory that dreaming helps us to sleep. If we didn't dream and release repressed emotions, the effects would continue lurking in the unconscious mind without an outlet and keep us awake. Once released via the dream, however, sleeping can resume (except intense anxiety dreams which sometimes keep us from going back to sleep for a spell). In a similar way, DTFs can be repressed material subject to analysis which make our day lighter.

Whether by free association, dreams, or meditation, those introspectively inclined can utilize the information revealed from patterns of DTFs. One example is the pattern of repetition of feelings of anger revealed over time, appearing as DTFs. One who was not consciously aware of anger until it was brought to consciousness can begin to reflect on its etiology and resolve anger issues that may have blocked his growth.

Another example of awareness of a pattern of DTFs is excessive self-blame and self-pity concerning chronic pain. The observing self, upon recognition of these negative charged emotions in meditation, can awaken to their existence. Then one has the opportunity to realize that these negative emotions may be hindering one from overcoming self-blame or self-pity. This opens the opportunity to take steps to reduce or eliminate these self-destructive thoughts and feelings.

Positive charged DTFs can lead to positive ideas, intuitions, and creativity. While Freud emphasized the pathogenic sexual and aggressive aspects of the human psyche, psychoanalyst Carl Jung added an appreciation of artistic and creative importations coming from the depths of the unconscious. Jung was interested in life-energizing "visions" coming out of the unconscious.

The English poet, Robert Browning, wrote that truth is within, and to know that truth consists in opening a way where the imprisoned splendor can escape. While Browning lived prior to psychoanalytic thinking and treatment, he was aware of creative gems coming from within which Carl Jung in a later time period interpreted as manifestations of the creative role of the unconscious.

Positive DTFs from meditation can bring creative manifestations such as those that came into the mind of Browning, Edison, and countless other thinkers, scientists, and artists. They did not have the benefits of psychoanalysis or meditation, but they were geniuses who could tap into the unconscious creative mind. Most of us are not geniuses, but those who meditate can have glimpses into creativity via distracting mind. This comes from the function of mind interferences to allow release of positive and negative effects from mind emptying, and moments of silence.

In my practice of meditation, mind distractions have often turned out to be creative ideas. For example, in the early days of my meditation practice I remember a period when I was overwhelmed with DTFs during a phase when I was trying to finish an article I was writing. My initial reaction towards these pesky intrusions during my meditations had been a cause for annoyance and frustration. After all, they were ostensibly preventing me from concentrating on my meditation object! But gradually I learned to rightfully reframe these distractions from a feeling a failure to a boon of gratefulness. The disturbances were actually inspired thoughts that I used to help me with ideas for the very article I was writing.

> "Those on the spiritual path are more likely to practice in a structured way. Because of their faith, discipline, motivation, and inspiration from their teachings as well as their leaders, they are more likely to withstand, adapt, and coexist with mind blockages."

DTFs and Personality Types

How prospective meditation aspirants will fare with DTF challenges will be influenced by personality styles. Let us ponder three personality types: those who are restless; those who are spontaneous; and those who like structure.

The restless type, the actively kinetic individual, is unlikely to tolerate DTFs. He runs around nonstop to accomplish daily goals. He is impatient with sitting in one position in the quiet. When confronted with mind obstacles he will fight to eliminate them. We know how impossible and frustrating that can be. He will conclude that meditation is a waste of time. He is more drawn to activities such as aerobics, bicycling, and running.

The spontaneous type springs into action at will. That is, he prefers to act when he is in the mood. He shuns scheduling. Instead of setting designated time periods to meditate, he does so at will, like someone who prefers to cook, read, and garden when he is in the mood, or a college student who studies at various times rather than being tied down to a set schedule. The spontaneous type often meditates when he is in a peaceful mood, since that is a time he is more likely to tolerate mind intrusions. His attitude is that it would be fruitless and counterproductive to keep sitting to tough it out in the presence of too many mental challenges. Yet, he can have a nonjudgmental attitude towards stopping. He will simply get up and try again another time to have a more productive experience. As they say in the army, it is not surrender, but a "tactical withdrawal." One of the big advantages of this approach is that it limits frustration time with distractions since, when too many mind distractions come on the scene, he bails out.

The structured type is big on organization. He meditates with a routine at the same time, daily, and for a set duration of time. Despite the onslaught of mental and physical DTFs, he is less likely to feel like a failure because he has at least succeeded in showing up and hanging in there, and being regular in his practice. By staying seated for a long time he has more experience and success reverting back to the meditation object. He also has more time to realize the benefits of mind obstructions.

Those on the spiritual path are more likely to practice in a structured way. Because of their faith, discipline, motivation, and inspiration from their teachings as well as their leaders, they are more likely to withstand, adapt, and coexist with mind blockages. This is reflected in the book *Beyond the Relaxation Response*, by Herbert Benson, MD. His tenet is that one's ability to stay the course in meditation is better if meditation is performed and practiced for spiritual reasons rather than for relaxation and stress avoidance. This is called the "faith factor."

Those in the restless, spontaneous, and structured categories may crossover into another category over time. Or, they can move out completely from their category to another. For example, a mildly restless personality may, for whatever reason, become less restless and move into the spontaneous category. Or, he may become interested in some type of meditation involving the body such as imagery, qigong, or movement oriented yoga. Even walking, washing the dishes, and gardening can be considered a form of meditation if there is a conscious attempt to stay in the present moment. This is a form of active mindfulness meditation. Witness meditation also may be an option for the restless personality, either as a meditation in itself or as a bridge to a spontaneous or structured stage.

Those in the spontaneous category may temporarily or permanently shift to the third type when they sense that they can progress further in meditation, by adding more structure. Even though I am mostly in the third category of structured time, I occasionally get up from sitting before my allotted time duration when totally frustrated by DTFs. This happens when I experience "dry" periods in meditation where I need to rest awhile from the routine. I temporarily move from the third type to the second type. I know that this is just a temporary deviation and I will come back again to my structured time soon thereafter.

Summary

In the thinking of western Psychotherapy, there are two major obstacles to staying with rudimentary meditation. First is frustration with the volume and tenacity of mind distractions. Second are upsetting emotions such as anger, anxiety, and fear from DTFS. Here are suggestions to overcome the barriers of discomfort, frustration, and discouragement from these obstacles.

In the early stages of meditation we must accept the fact that mind distractions are unavoidable, and that peaceful coexistence rather than futile battle is the right expectation and goal.

Coping with mind distractions is a laboratory for training in controlling mind and feelings during meditation practice and in daily life. Reduce the volume of mind disturbances whenever possible by not rushing into meditation after busy mind activities such as intense work or play. Brief relaxation techniques prior to meditation, such as deep breathing, qigong, and imagery, can reduce the volume of mind challenges.

Additionally, one can familiarize oneself with the patterns of mental involvement. For example, are they thoughts and feelings? Are they positive or negative? Are they about the present, past, or future? Knowing the nature of these patterns by labeling them will help one recognize their appearance and dismiss them faster.

Distractions empty the mind by flushing out the clutter of stored and repetitive matter. This ultimately fosters better concentration on the meditation object, and more freedom from clutter both during meditation times and during the normal day.

Mind disturbances, without our even noticing them, can bring on split second moments of silence between the time of recognition and acknowledgment of the distraction, and the return to the meditation object.

Mind interferences themselves can be positive and creative importations from the conscious and unconscious mind, resulting in intuition, creativity, and guidance.

Disturbing thoughts and feelings often release into awareness repressed feelings. For those who are introspective, their revelation can open up a new dimension of understanding leading to emotional growth and freedom, all similar to the benefits derived in psychoanalysis and dream interpretation.

Finally, one's personality type and meditational goals will be a factor in how one tolerates and manages mental interruptions.

In conclusion, our chances of staying on course with meditation are greatly enhanced by the strategies to deal with mind distractions as set forth in this article. Particularly important is the understanding that mind distractions themselves can bring benefits to the meditation process. Even if one experiences mind disturbances in the majority of one's meditation, the result will be achieving something important. Whenever one achieves the major goal of focusing on one's meditation object, one will end up feeling productive and enthusiastic. And, when one is unable to stay focused even in the midst of mental interference, while realizing the value of these mind interruptions, one will still come away feeling sufficiently productive, adequate to the task, and confident.

> "....one's ability to stay the course in meditation is better if meditation is performed and practiced for spiritual reasons rather than for relaxation and stress avoidance. This is called the 'faith factor.'"

Michael S. Isaacs is a psychotherapist in private practice in San Francisco, California. He has a Bachelor of Arts degree from Cornell University in history; a Doctorate in Law from New York University; a Master's degree in social work from Case Western University; and a national certification as a psychoanalyst from the New Jersey Institute of Psychoanalysis. He has a special interest in the relationship between psychotherapy and spirituality. When appropriate, he will introduce spiritual truths and values into the psychotherapy process to solve problems and enhance creativity.

◆ Helen Appell

Charya Nritya
Nepalese Buddhist Dance of Deity Yoga

The Kathmandu Valley in Nepal lies at the crossroads of the ancient civilizations of Asia. Legend holds that the area was once covered by a lake. Nepal Mandala, as the Kathmandu Valley was known, was created by the divine intervention of the altruistic deity Manjushri, the great Mahayana and Tantric bodhisattva.

Using his flaming sword that cuts through ignorance, this lord of wisdom sliced a gorge that drained the lake and created a lush valley suitable for human habitation. The Newars are the earliest known and, hence by all evidence, original inhabitants of the valley.

As Manjushri's divine land, Nepal Mandala gave rise to a profoundly rich culture of spiritual wisdom and sacred arts. These arts serve as offerings to the vast pantheon of Buddhist and Hindu divinities and provide esoteriological methods to awaken the deity within both artist and appreciator.

The Dance of the Deities

The dance form known as *Charya Nritya*, a Sanskrit term translatable as "dance as a spiritual discipline," is a Newar Buddhist movement practice that originated a thousand years ago in the Kathmandu Valley. The esoteric purpose of the dance is to bring a bodily dimension to the meditator's usual sitting practice of "deity yoga" and, in a ritual setting, to enable the dancer to fully become the deity in body, speech, and mind in order to benefit all beings. In its traditional context, the initiated observers of Charya Nritya could experience the blessings and presence of the Buddhist deities bodied forth in the dances.

The tradition of Charya dance consists of many individual dances, each one representing a particular deity drawn from the vast pantheon of Buddhist bodhisattvas, dakinis (feminine wisdom beings), and manifestations of Buddha. Every aspect of a dance item expresses the character and mood of that specific deity, including the color of the costume, the ornaments, gestures, movement style, postures, energy level, and associated props. Examples of regularly performed deities would include Green *Tara*, with her all-accomplishing compassionate activity; *Vajrayogini*, her red intensity transforming passion into discriminating wisdom; and dark blue *Vajrapani*, embodiment of purified wrath, fiercely protecting the practitioner from the poison of ego clinging.

Newar Buddhists believe that humans are divine in their deepest nature, but have not awakened to this realization. A shift of awareness in relationship to body, speech, and mind is what reveals the deity within. The mystery of this transformation can only emerge through the union of the triune aspects of mudra ('wisdom seal'), a complete experience of embodiment. The significance of this intimate relationship of Body-Speech-Mind, as well as the richness and complexity of the symbolic language, is narrated and demonstrated in this highly informative and experiential ritual dance performance. It is important to remember that Charya dance is more spiritual practice than performance art.

The songs (*charya giti*) that accompany the dance describe and praise the appearance, gestures (mudras), and qualities of each specific deity. Mainly sung in Sanskrit with sparse instrumental accompaniment, the lyrics provide the primary guidance for the dancers' mudras. The dancer moves in a graceful *tribhanga* (three part) posture, with the hip and head slightly tilted, a stance frequently seen in the iconography of Buddhist thangkas (embroidered paintings) and statuary. From this base, the dancer continuously expresses a subtle wave of movement while maintaining a meditative, inward-looking focus. In this process the dancer becomes the deity through the non-dual interplay of giving and receiving.

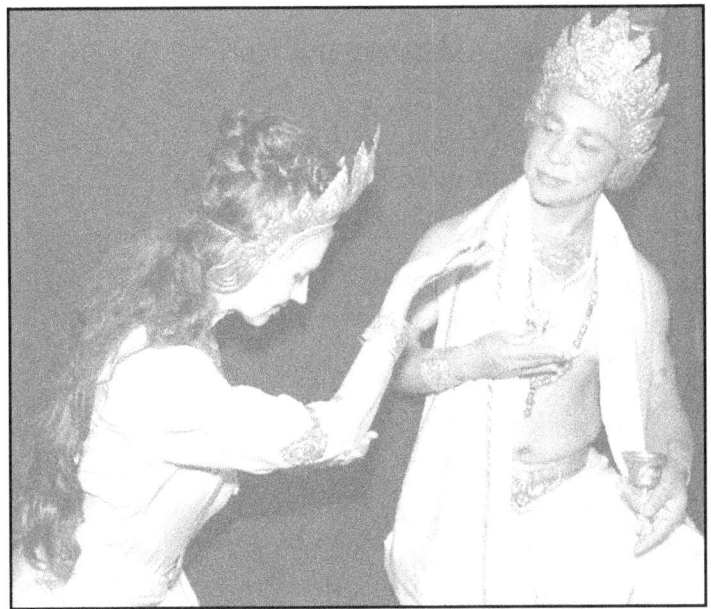

As seen in the sacred paintings and statues, every deity sits or stands with his or her head, hands, and feet in specific positions and with distinctive facial expressions. Through observing Charya Nritya, the viewer can discover that the deity's body represented in sacred art forms is not static, but rather a dynamic unfolding of expressive movement.

The universe of a divine being, the surrounding environment, or mandala, is also experienced as divine. As the dancers become the deities, everything and everyone that surrounds them is ultimately experienced as the divine world. The audience becomes an intimate part of their world, sharing the *rasa*, the "taste," or essence, of each sacred movement.

Colors in this ritual realm correspond to the most fundamental universal energies, those of the five elements: earth, water, fire, air, and space. A perfect elemental balance is central to the yogic practice of deity meditation and hence integral to the Charya dances, in which the colors worn are also considered mudra. For example, golden yellow expresses the earth element, which in ideal balance with the other elements carries an abundance in nutrients that bestow nourishment in the form of abundant crops, wealth, and overall prosperity and, beyond these more worldly but nonetheless important planes, fullness of spiritual practice. A single bold color can represent a universe in the tiniest speck of dirt, or the loftiest and subtlest attainment of wisdom.

The ritual dancer's ornaments, too, are deeply symbolic. Six articles of jewelry adorning six parts of the body reflect the beauty of transcendent qualities, the six paramitas. The deities' necklaces express generosity, while bracelets and anklets represent morality and self-discipline. The earrings symbolize patience, and the sash around the waist speaks of determination and joyful effort. The marking for the third eye signifies meditative concentration, while the crown, with its five jewels (or five skulls for wrathful deities) convey the harmonious completeness of the wisdoms of the five Buddha families. The same ornamental decorations of the Charya meditator are found in the sacred paintings and statues of the embodied and portrayed deities.

The hands and arms purify space through repeated motions followed by gestures such as those of compassionate generosity or drinking the nectar of enlightenment, depending on the divine quality embodied. The legs, on their own plane of relating to the earth, command attention and define the circle of the deity's mandala, being the foundation for all enlightened activity. Expressiveness also comes through the dancer's spiritual intentions. A performer-meditator may shake with the intensity of energy required to face and shift all unwholesome states of mind and overcome negative interferences on the spiritual path.

The hand gesture mudras are extremely important. Some are easily intuited, such as the often seen *bhumi sparsha mudra*, (earth touching gesture) of Buddha Shakyamuni's enlightenment, with the right hand touching the earth and the left hand resting at the navel in meditative poise. Some mudras literally point to the right and left hands, such as in the "two hands" gesture. Here the right (male energy) symbolizes conventional reality and skillful activity, and the left (female energy) symbolizes absolute reality and foundational wisdom.

The long-term and more gradual benefits of mudra cannot directly be observed during a performance, but they are the ultimate purpose of this meditation. Over time the practitioner's body is carved and sculpted by the poses and movements, a gracious expressive quality of speech is released, and the mind's universal awareness is slowly unveiled. Mudras can liberate the energy of negative habits and remove their damaging effects. Fully inhabiting the body deeply affects the mind. For a Charya dancer, the energetic interplay of the mudras of body, speech, and mind becomes the entire universe, "the dance of life," on the principle that as you move, you become, and what you become you express, making it possible for others to experience and respond. Thus, a practitioner of Charya Nritya becomes a student of Buddhist iconography, kinesthetic energetics, human emotion, Sanskrit language, meditation, and divine qualities.

The Master Dancer and Dance Mandal

Buddhist priest and consummate Charya dancer, Prajwal Ratna Vajracharya, established Dance Mandal — Foundation for

the Preservation of the Sacred Arts of Nepal in Kathmandu in 1996. Four years later, Prajwal moved to Portland, Oregon and undertook the challenge of transplanting and transmitting his highly stylized ritual dance form in a western context.

Prajwal Ratna Vajracharya began his training in this meditative dance ritual at the age of eight, receiving teachings mainly from his father, the renowned Buddhist priest and scholar Ratna Kaji Vajracharya. Prajwal has dedicated his life to his father's vision of preserving this sacred art form as Nepal adapts to the changes of the 21st century. Prajwal has set out to expand this ritual dance while maintaining its profoundly spiritual intention. Prajwal and Dance Mandal bring Charya Nritya from the hidden sacred spaces of the temples of Nepal to a range of public venues around the world.

Charya Nritya is a beautifully moving and compelling artistic expression of the Newar Buddhist belief that our own human state — our body, speech, and mind — is the foundation for the attainment and manifestation of divine activity. Indeed, in the Newar view, this is the ultimate purpose of human life.

Helen Appell is a student of Prajwal Ratna Vajracharya. She studied and practiced Vajrayana Buddhism in India, and spent years in monastic practice as a Zen priest. Helen found integration and expression through the study, practice, teaching, and performing of Charya Nritya. In 2009, Prajwal and Helen together founded Nritya Mandala Mahavihara, a Newar Buddhist temple complex in Portland, Oregon to teach, practice, and perform the dance in the traditional ritual environment. Her wish for Dance Mandal is to share the joy of dance in temples and centers throughout the world.

Recognition

Ah, Great Mystery
We cannot enter You,
nor from You can we escape
We're held in thrall, as if enchanted
You are so close we overlook You

Not an object to be gained...
Already within our very nature...
This sounds too good to be true, too easy
So we doubt,
and make excuses for our ignorance

We wax poetic and philosophize
Attempting conquest and capture
You, without corners, unbound by concepts
Continue to slip through our fingers

How can we know You, Great Unknown?
The wisest say "abandon trying"
For what we seek is that which seeks

True recognition, how marvelous!

DS Lokanath

Swami Aseshananda

THE AWAKENING OF POWER
Beyond Intellectualism, Spirituality

By the word "power," and unless otherwise stated, Swami Aseshananda most always spoke about the spiritual variety, as instanced when he once said, *"Science has split the atom and released a great power for destruction. But Sri Ramakrishna came to split the curtain of maya in order to free all beings from the suffering caused by destruction."* On another occasion, clarifying the distinction but without mentioning any names, he once declared: *"Those who want power get Rolls Royces; those who want peace get God."*

The subject of my talk this morning to the western people is the Awakening of Power. The western civilization is predominantly a dualistic civilization. And its two sources of power are: intellectualism, given by the Greek philosophers like Plato and Aristotle; and Judaism, that is Judaism that has given to the western civilization its monotheistic idea of God and man. In other words, this intellectualism creates a dualism between subject and object. And the theological tradition of the West also creates another type of dualism — call it spiritual dualism. In spiritual dualism there will always remain a distinction between man and God, even when a man has attained salvation.

By the way, salvation is a postmortem experience. The West does not interpret it in line with attaining jivanmukti, liberation. I preach only jivanmukti to all of you. You may not be able to understand it properly now, but someday you will understand. When I declare jivanmukti, then you will have to create a distinction between the apparent self and the real Self. This is a fresh type of dualism, if you will. When you think of your apparent self, you think in terms of distinction. America is not England. England is not France. So when we make this distinction between ego and Atman, we are making it based on our individuality. And this individuality is finite. So as long as you have this finite individuality you will not be a jivanmukta. You have got another individuality, which I call infinite individuality. That is Advaita Vedanta. And Swami Vivekananda came to give to the western people this Advaita. Be a jivanmukta.

In how many places did Swami Vivekananda give this idea to the western man; many have listened, few have tried to practice it. In other words, in order to be a jivanmukta you cannot think in terms of the reality of the world. The West has accepted the world to be real. Why? Because the people here are taught that God created the world.

Take for example, the Book of Genesis. Five thousand years ago, say, on Friday afternoon (laughter), God said *"Let there be light."* And there was light, called the Creation. But what occurred prior to that, and after tomorrow? It must be that behind this manifested universe there is a supreme intelligence. But if we say this, we must declare that this supreme intelligence is a distinct intelligence from individual consciousness. Here, mere intellectualism will not help. Intellectualism creates a distinction between subject and the object. Through intellect you can know only the appearance of man, not the real of man.

Namarupa means name and form. When I say I know you, I know your name is Tom, Dick, or Harry. Is this the real man? And what is the definition of Reality? The definition of reality is "That which never changes." Now, take for example, Aristotle. His work was accepted by Thomas Aquinas, like Aristotle's philosophy and bible.

Thomas Aquinas tried to bridge the gulf between reason and faith. Faith prevailed through the Middle Ages; faith in revelation, faith in the scripture, especially the Bible. But after the Renaissance, science became the tool for opening the door of wisdom for western man. Then came the 18th century philosophers, called rationalists. Jefferson was very much inspired by the rationalism of the European philosophers in the 18th century, and due to this he gave the American people its great ideal: life, liberty, and the pursuit of happiness.

Now, when one thinks of life, liberty, and the pursuit of happiness, one is thinking in terms of an affluent society. In order to create an affluent society you need science and technology. When you take to science and technology, you create machines.

But man wants something more. Man wants freedom. He is not satisfied with political freedom, or social freedom, or economic freedom. He wants to be free from the tyranny of nature.

Nature brings three messengers to control man: disease, old age, and death. But man, if he is not illumined, falls a victim. In other words, he gets depressed, he feels weak. Therefore, the real power in man comes not through accomplishments like success in external life. The power in man comes when man becomes the master of nature. By controlling external nature science has developed tremendously. And therefore, science has been able to say that we can go to the moon.

But science has not been able to give the western man its real dignity, its real heritage, its real *"pearl of great price,"* because science cannot answer this question, "why?" Its answer, up to now, has been, "how?" Why is this universe? Science will say the "big bang." Who caused the big bang? They will say, "Black Hole." You see, when you are interpreting in a scientific way you are bound to use a mechanistic interpretation. But you should know this: you will not find a trace of Consciousness anywhere in the external world of time, space, and causation.

Einstein has given this scientific world a tremendous power and prestige by discovering the equation. What is that equation? The equation is Energy = Mass x C₂. This refers to the 186,000 miles per second speed of light. And another observation he made was that there are different types of light: ultraviolet light, cosmic rays, etc. But here I ask this question: Does your science answer the question of why you are here? You might say, "But swami, that is not the field of science. We want to know how we can live here comfortably, peacefully, and probably with a little bit of influence and power over nature." I would answer, "Is this all?" And that is the reason the Indian philosophers bring up *Aparavidya*; you have specialized in lower knowledge.

Now India, in spite of its ignorance, poverty, and present religious superstition, has created a Ramakrishna. He stands for *Paravidya*. What is Paravidya? Knowledge of the indestructible Reality by which you will be able to conquer death and attain immortality here and now. Therefore, we encounter the path of renunciation. Here, in the West, you have combined bhoga and yoga — enjoyment and practice — accepting the philosophy of the Jewish tradition.

But Sri Ramakrishna has come to teach to you renounce, renounce, renounce. Why renounce? To attain perfection; to attain jivanmukti; to attain immortality. What do you renounce, then? Renounce your egocentric consciousness, renounce your selfishness, renounce your greed, renounce your pride, renounce your hatred.

You see, right now the Liberal Party in South Africa is thinking in terms of sanctions. This will not solve the problem. As long as you see difference between white and black, as long as you see difference between East and West; so long you will want to explode the whole universe with your atom bombs.

There are two great superpowers who are creating a tremendous confusion; one is America, the other is Russia [This discourse was given in 1986]. I tell these two super powers to renounce all your atom bombs; you are creating nuclear difficulties. Not by atom bombs, not by nuclear bomb, but by understanding and following the method of humanism, by following the method of spirituality, by following the method of building an inner life and a strong foundation, by producing jivanmuktas, illumined souls who will be the leaders of your society, the leaders of your civilization, leaders of your culture, then you will live up to the message of Christ.

Christ preached renunciation. Because I was a student in St. Paul's Cathedral Mission College, the words of Christ created a tremendous urge in my mind to renounce the world and live a life of dedication for realizing the Truth and telling it to any person who would listen. For passing the examination I used to read the Bible very carefully. But after joining the Ramakrishna Order I read between the lines of the Bible and found Christ's real message — especially in the Sermon on the Mount.

The central message of Christ is renounce and realize God in this lifetime, and then be an asset to humanity. Because at one time Christ said, "....*though they wanted bread, you are giving them stones.*" Theology, doctrines, and creeds, to me, are mere stones. Your life and religion should not be merely preached, it is to be lived. And holy life will never come to any man unless he practices renunciation everyday, every moment of his life.

What are you to renounce then? Three things you are to renounce. I go to Shankara for the teaching. You have to renounce your desires for perpetuating this samsara. This samsara has come on account of unfulfilled desire; that means, it is unfulfilled desire that has brought you here. And avidya, focus on lower knowledge, is the cause because you have forgotten your real self. That is, you are identifying yourself with your apparent self. And this life will end in death and you do not know where you are going. Your future is unknown and the present is uncertain. And this is the predicament of man. But in this predicament man can solve his problem by transcending the limited intellectual plane of consciousness. Your intellectualism will not give you penetration into the heart of Reality.

And that is the reason why Sri Ramakrishna's message is to transcend intellectualism, transcend this dualistic philosophy of life which creates a distinction between man and God. And that is what he taught to Swami Vivekananda. Swami Vivekananda was intellectually bright, but he did not believe in the existence of God. He was in those days fascinated by Herbert Spencer. Herbert Spencer is known as one of the great agnostics.

And therefore, Swamiji's question to Sri Ramakrishna and other teachers was, "*Sir, have you seen God?*" He went to the Brahmo Samaj teacher, Devendranath Tagore, who said to him, "*Young man, you have got brilliant eyes.*" Swamiji replied, "*What shall I do with brilliant eyes? Please answer my question sir.*" Tagore then quoted from the Upanisads. But Swamiji then told him, "*Sir, I am not satisfied with the quotation from this scripture or that scripture. I want to know whether any person has realized God.*" But when he came to Ramakrishna, the great Master said, "*Young man, not only I have seen God, but I can also help you to see God. The method is viveka and vairagya.*"

Viveka really means that everything is changeful and vairagya means renounce your attachment to the changeful things of the universe and discover the Reality which never changes. Realize God, realize your true Self, realize a state of consciousness which is beyond intellect, beyond time, space, and causation, beyond the world of maya, beyond the world of namarupa — name and form. Thereafter Sri Ramakrishna told Swami Vivekananda to keep his intellect but purify his intellect and transcend intellect.

When we are in the intellectual plane, then we know only maya. Maya does not mean illusion; maya means appearance. And it is based on your apparent self or ego. When I say I'm a Hindu, or you say you are an American, it is the ego that is speaking. But behind the ego there is the Atman, the real Self. The real Self of every man, whether eastern man or western man, is infinite Consciousness.

Sri Ramakrishna uses the example called the salt doll. Ego can be compared with a salt doll. And the salt doll is not happy because there is a gregarious instinct in every other salt doll. Man is a social being so he cannot be happy when he is alone. He wants companionship with other people. Now you ask one salt doll, what is the source from which you have come? What is your origin? The salt doll will say, "My origin is Salt Lake City. I've come from Salt Lake City." But an illumined teacher will teach that this Salt Lake City origin is a relative truth. He will tell you that your origin is something else. Then he will take the salt doll to the Pacific Ocean. And when the salt doll sees the ocean, his true origin, he will want to measure the depth of that ocean. The moment it touches the ocean, however, it dissolves. What does this mean? That as long as you identify with your salt doll nature, you will never know your real nature. In order to know your real nature you must renounce your sense of finitude, renounce your attachment to nama-rupa, name and form. So, we must discover our real nature, which is the essence; essence of the universe, the essence of my psycho-physical being which is called the Atman.

And what is the nature of the Atman? For that you have to read the Upanisads. In the Katho Upanisad, the question is what happens to man when he dies? That is the question, which Nachiketas asked Yama. Yama was the teacher. A student is ignorant. He has to go to an illumined teacher to understand the meaning of life, the purpose of life, the goal of life, and how to attain that goal. Nachiketas asked him, *"What happens to a man when he dies?"* Yama replied, *"This is a very difficult question; even the gods in heaven are puzzled by it. Ask me some other question."* But Nachiketas was imbued with the spirit of renunciation and did not waver. Yama said, *"I will give you long life, I will give you damsels, I will give you pleasures of the senses, music, and entertainment,"* Nachiketas replied, *"Dancing, singing, merrymaking be yours; I am not interested in entertainment. I am interested in attainment of the Truth which will make me immortal."*

Then Yama, the teacher, said, *"There are two paths: the path of shreyas and the path of preyas. The path of preyas means the path of happiness. If you seek that path your happiness will come, but it will also go away. But if you seek the path of illumination then you have to renounce your attachment to the vanities of life. Then you will be thinking in terms of permanent happiness which is eternal."*

But you cannot reach that happiness unless you have transcended the plane of the intellect. And in order to transcend the plane of intellect, the samskaras of the subconscious mind must be purified. Your conscious mind must come under your control. And then, through the grace of the guru, through the grace of the personal god, you'll be able to open the door to the super conscious. And when you reach the superconscious state of light and enlightenment you'll realize the truth just as surely as a fruit in the palm of your hand. It is spiritual experience alone that can teach man that God is real, not by intellectual understanding, or by acceptance of a creed or faith or a dogma, or even a kind of theological understanding of men and things of the world.

In the Indian tradition we have satsanga, keeping company with illumined souls, and taking instruction from an illumined teacher. What I can say for myself is that Holy Mother blessed me and gave me the key to the realization of God in the form of the mantra. Therefore, there should be guru shakti first. The western tradition is that I must belong to the church and follow the doctrines of the church, and they will be the source of my inspiration. But not in Indian tradition. It is a kind of close relationship between the teacher and the student that is most important.

The teacher must be brilliant, must be well accomplished. He must be like a specialist. You see, when you go to an M.D., he tries this medicine, that medicine, and so on. Nothing works. Then what do you do? You go to a specialist. This is the case of the student and the teacher in spiritual life.

But always remember that all compounded things are subject to decay. Trouble is bound to come to any person who has a body. You have to pay a little tax on it, you see. The tax is disease, old age, and death. What will they teach us? They teach us be detached, be detached from the body. Not only the body, but detached from the mind. It is relatively easy to be detached from the body, but difficult to be detached from the mind. And finally you must be detached from your personal self, ego.

The Indian tradition speaks of the three bodies. As long as you are alive you want to preserve your gross body. But at the time of death everything is not over. You identify with your subtle body, which you call "soul." It is the soul that goes here and there, different places, but it comes back to earth because this is called the *karma bhumi*, the plane of cause and effect. You may go to heaven and hear some nice songs, like angels singing and all of that, but you have also gone to heaven on account of the effect of your past karma. It is a world of name and form too. When the effect is exhausted there, then you come back here. This is reincarnation in samsara. But in the Indian tradition, you can attain illumination, moksha.

All of this is based upon the theological concept of the Christian faith, which is called sin and salvation. But the Indian way of thinking is not sin and salvation, it is samsara and nirvana. Buddha used those words, samsara and nirvana. Samsara means coming into this merry-go-round of the world. It's called a wheel; birth, death, and rebirth — the wheel of samsara. But when you stop that wheel, then there is nirvana. Nirvana means Atmajnanam, you realize your true nature to be infinite consciousness, infinite wisdom, infinite life, and infinite spirit. Until then, you are the infinite spirit dreaming finite dreams. So wake up! Wake up from this dream! Ignorance is compared to a dream. As long as the dream lasts, our experiences seem real. But when you wake up, they are seen to be unreal. All the troubles will be over when you awaken your consciousness from this relative truth, from *vyavaharika*, the world of time, space, and causation.

Therefore, Einstein or any great scientist will never be able to give the solution for the problem of death, or for realizing the truth of immortality. Sri Ramakrishna can teach these. Holy Mother can teach these. Swami Vivekananda can teach these. Swami Vivekananda liked to quote this verse from the Taittiriya Upanisad: *"There is a state of Consciousness called Turiya, the transcendental state of Consciousness."* The common experiences of every man are in the waking state. Then at night he goes into the state of dream. The subject/object difference will remain in these two states. In a dream he will find that he is seeing some object, meeting some friend, because mind is connected to the nervous system. Even in dream the nervous system is working.

When does the nervous system stop working? In the state of deep sleep. In deep sleep, called *sushupti*, there is no kind of dualistic experience of subject and object. So these three states belong to time. But if you can transcend the three states, you can reach Turiya, the fourth state, which is known as Samadhi.

> "Your conscious mind must come under your control. And then, through the grace of the guru, through the grace of the personal god, you'll be able to open the door to the super conscious. And when you reach the superconscious state of light and enlightenment you'll realize the truth just as surely as a fruit in the palm of your hand."

Buddha called it Nirvana. Christian mystics called it Beatific Vision.

So, you have another kind of experience, called timeless. When Shakespeare said time must have stopped, it is not only time, but the law of causation also stops; also space stops, because time, space, and causation are three categories that belong to the *vijnanamaya kosha*. When we lift our consciousness to the intellectual plane, then time, space, and causation will seem real. Scientists have not transcended time, space, and causation. There's a book out, a kind of dialogue between J. Krishnamurti and David Bohm, and the title of the book is called *The Ending of Time*. Now, scientists have come to the conclusion that time is relative, but the end of time all scientists have not accepted. The idea that time/space is relative is Einstein's great contribution. But nuclear physicists like Max Planck or Niels Bohr, and especially Heisenberg, are talking to the scientists and saying that the law of causation is also relative, because causation is based in mathematics.

But the western civilization depending upon mathematics for precision is like a tire that has sprung a leak. Mathematics cannot give certainty, it can give only probability. What is certainty then? For that you have to go to the East. And there you will hear, "*I am Consciousness.*" You can deny everything, but you cannot deny the existence of the denier. Yet, over that truism of "I am Consciousness," the ego is always superimposing "I am an American," or "I am a Hindu," or "I am a Christian," or "I'm an agnostic," or "I'm a Republican." But these are all upadhis, coverings. Even in the Bible you read, "*I am that I am.*" When you identify with prakriti, nature, you create problems. So isolate yourself from prakriti, then you will realize your true nature to be eternal and not mortal; your true nature to be infinite, not finite; your true nature to be divine, not sinful.

So, anything in this world of time is bound to be destroyed. But man becomes great when he has conquered time. How can he conquer time? When he conquers his ego. When you wake up from this dream and realize that your real nature is infinite, then time is cut away. The end of time will come with enlightenment. An illumined soul alone can teach that; not scientists, nor theologians, nor a faithful devotee of a dualistic philosophy.

So this is the thing, until you conquer time you are tossed in the waves of maya. Maya means happiness and misery. That means you identify yourself with vritti chaitanya. That insight is a gift of Kapila. When you know anything through your intellect you are identifying with the waves of the mind, because one thought brings another thought.

And therefore, a person of discrimination will practice detachment from the thought waves of the mind and identify with the Purusha; Purusha means background Consciousness. Therefore, you have to make a distinction between vritti chaitanya and svarupa chaitanya; svarupa chaitanya means the property. The property of Consciousness does not belong to mind. The property of Consciousness belongs to your real Self.

Your apparent self is the body. But when you identify with the body, your existence will be connected with the appearance, nama-rupa; your existence will be connected with the flesh, not with the Spirit. It is the same with the subtle body as well as the causal body. Ego creates the mind, mind creates the body. When you transcend the ego you realize all pervading Consciousness, or infinite Consciousness, your true nature. Our body is only a symbol of existence, and mind is a symbol of consciousness. And consciousness is always connected with infinite Consciousness, not with finite consciousness. Finite consciousness will be always changeful. Infinite Consciousness will always be changeless.

Everything that you know through the intellect, or anything that we experience in this empirical world of time, space, and causation is fleeting, is changeful, is in constant flux. From the scientific point of view the solidarity of the world is gone, is a mass of energy. Swamiji spoke about that to Nikola Tesla. He said, "You have converted energy into mass or matter. Now, can you convert matter or mass into energy?" Nikola Tesla said that he could, and asked Swamiji to come to his laboratory the next Monday. Swamiji went. But Tesla did not have the equation, which Einstein discovered through his fine brain. He could not accomplish what Swamiji asked of him.

But the real equation, if you ask Swamiji, is don't start with Reality if you think Reality is equal to nature as computed by thought. My equation will be, Reality is equal to man transcendent of thought. If a western scientist would say that matter is akin to consciousness via thought, then he would transcend the scientific plane. He would become a mystic. But here is not just mysticism, it is realization, nirvikalpa samadhi. That is why Swami Brahmananda says in the *Eternal Companion*, "*Show me the line of demarcation where matter ends and spirit begins.*"

There seem to be two things: matter and Spirit. In the sense plane it is all matter. In samadhi, in the transcendent, it is all Spirit. In actuality there are not two. Matter, mind, soul — these concepts are meaningful in the relative plane, but in the absolute plane there is only Consciousness. That is why we say, "No mind, no matter. No matter? Never mind!" Anything that is changeful, that must be called material. Only the unchanging or unchangeable principle of Consciousness is called spirit, or Atman.

So, you will find that your consciousness is singular, never dual or plural. To reach this consciousness, your true nature, the Katho Upanisad tells us that we have to search in the cave of the heart. Do not seek without, but seek within. Man is like a musk deer. He is searching for that wonderful fragrance in the forest, on the outside; but happiness is within, like the musk in a deer's navel. But in the West you are projecting that happiness on your friend, on your wealth, on your property, or on your beautiful car, Mercedes car or Cadillac car — you are always projecting.

But the source of happiness is within when you realize that your true nature is a sun that always shines. The sun never loses the power of shining but moon shines by borrowed light. Similarly, mind is like the moon. If you identify with the mind, your happiness will be precarious. Identify with the sun; it is always shining — although here in Portland you don't see the face of the sun for many days [laughter].

But that does not mean the sun is not shining. As the sun cannot live without its brilliant power, similarly a man of illumination cannot live without identifying himself with his infinite Spirit, which is deathless, which is birthless, which is eternal, and which is ever free.

So here we find that in order to understand what the Vedanta is saying, you must attain peace of mind. Your mind is restless, so calmness of mind is necessary. First, you have to create one wave. That means *ekagrata*, one-pointed mind. I belong to God. God loves me and I love God. I'll bend all my efforts to realize God. When you establish a relationship with God like this, you are following what is called bhakti marga, the path of devotion. But ultimate realization is called advaita jnana, where there is no distinction between I and my God.

Take for example the case of Sri Ramakrishna. First he realized God in His personal aspect, when he was performing tantra sadhana. He felt, I belong to God and God belongs to me. I can live without food, but I cannot live without my Mother. This relationship was so strong, so vivid in the mind of Sri Ramakrishna, that Sri Ramakrishna as an individual, separate from the Mother, disappeared. Once on Kali Puja night, the devotees saw there was no image of Mother Kali, but Sri Ramakrishna himself became Mother Kali, and Surendra Mitra offered flowers to Him, looking upon Sri Ramakrishna as the Divine Mother, the Mother of all mankind, the Mother of the Universe.

The Master used the Mother as the dynamic aspect. Christ used the Father. Whether you use father or mother, it means the personal aspect of God. The West has accepted the personal aspect, for when they say "God the Father" it means the personal aspect of God, the unmoved mover. That means the final cause. But the East speaks about Nirguna Brahman without attributes, formless, because the personal God cannot be the solution of all problems. It is not the Original.

The original source is Nirguna Brahman. That is the reason why the West has not been able to produce religious harmony. There is a kind of distinction between Judaism and Christianity. The distinction will remain as long as the Christian faith does not think in terms of a state of consciousness where there is no duality, because Judaism or Islam or any Semitic religion cannot accept the doctrine of Avatar —Divine Incarnation.

Jewish people will not accept the doctrine of divine incarnation. So, I will not speak of Sri Ramakrishna as a divine incarnation to them. I may talk of it to you, those who are devotees of Ramakrishna, but not to a Jewish person unless he accepts Sri Ramakrishna as his chosen ideal. That is a different story. You should not disturb the faith of others. If I am to talk to a scientist like David Bohm, I will not talk about Sri Ramakrishna as a divine incarnation; I would speak in terms of advaita. You scientists, you think that you have known everything? You do not know anything unless you have realized the Atman. So practice renunciation. Join this monastery, I will teach you [laughter].

In the book I mentioned earlier, David Bohm asked very brilliant questions. Krishnamurti was equally good. But in the eastern tradition an illumined guru is necessary. Krishnamurti does not think so. So we agree to disagree on that point. Shankara says that the shastra must be interpreted by an illumined guru. If the illumined guru interprets it, then it will ring a bell in your heart. If a mere scholar interprets, it will not change your life. So there is a big difference there, but it is all right. Krishnamurti has done good work in this country because he has given an intellectual stimulation to the American people. The American people have become a little Atma-centered on account of Krishnamurti's teaching. He has given independence that you can become illumined. He says that you need not have a guru. Ultimately, your mind will become the guru, that is true, but the tradition has it that the guru is a necessity. The guru is a state of consciousness. But Krishnamurti thinks guru is a person. And we will create allegiance to a person and be like blind followers.

But that is not the point. An illumined guru does not want to make blind followers. Guru epitomizes the method, and so the illumined guru asks the student to follow the method. He never says I can do everything for you. He says I will show you the way, but you have to follow that way.

That is what Sri Ramakrishna said. He said, test this coin. I have realized God in His nirguna aspect, and have attained nirvikalpa samadhi. You too, must realize nirvikalpa samadhi. And that is the reason Swamiji was so anxious, so eager. But I will say it was through the grace of Sri Ramakrishna that he attained it. It was not through his own sadhana. It was not on account of his purity of life. The guru is like a bridge between the personal aspect and impersonal aspect of God. It is only through the grace of guru that one will be able to cross the boundary line between Nirguna Brahman and Saguna Brahman. Swamiji tried hard in all possible ways, but he failed. Then he said, "How long shall I wait? I cannot wait even a single second more." Seeing that eagerness, Sri Ramakrishna went into a higher state of consciousness, and from that higher state of consciousness said, "Tomorrow you will have it."

So when you know the word "guru," that means you will reach your higher state of consciousness and identify him with God. And it is God who speaks through the illumined guru, or an avatar. When Christ spoke the Sermon on the Mount, he was in samadhi. But it is not so much mentioned there. But here in Indian tradition, when an avatar comes, his natural state of consciousness is samadhi, Turiya — the fourth state of consciousness. He brings his mind down to the relative plane in order that human beings will be profited by his instruction and raise their consciousness from the relative world to the

– continued on page 59

◆ Paravasta Sam Bailey

SWAMI VIVEKANANDA
and the Eternal Brahman

The presence, teachings, and overall influence of Swami Vivekananda on the lives of contemporary people — monks, devotees, the layman, the youth of India, and now, the world — is an unprecedented phenomena of the rarest spiritual variety. As knowledge of his recent advent grows, humanity turns to embrace its Divine Nature.

If I understand correctly, the Middle Way suggests a correct view between the extremes of Nihilism and Eternalism. Some Buddhists say that the idea of Brahman is incorrect, because nothing is permanent, so the idea of Brahman is an example of Eternalism. I think these Buddhists are mistaken about what is the original, intended understanding of the Middle Way. It cannot be that the intention was to deny the existence of an eternal, unchanging Principle, for even Buddhism admits of such — variously named the Deathless nature, Buddha nature, Dharmakaya, or Rigpa (primordial, simple Awareness). Even the Theravadin teacher, Ajaan Maha Boowa, admits that *"This vanishes, that vanishes, but that which knows their vanishing remains."*

In the great Mahayana *Uttaratantra Shastra,* Maitreya states (through the instrumentality of his devotee Asanga) that Buddha Nature has four qualities: Purity, Bliss, Permanency, and Great Self (as opposed to Jivatman). This sounds like a perfect description of Brahman, and even seems to contradict certain interpretations of what Buddhism calls *Anatman.* What has caused me to wonder, is that the Buddha himself is recorded in the Pali Canon as saying that consciousness is impermanent, not eternal.

Consciousness as a Word first, then as a State

As the Vedanta states that Brahman is pure consciousness, and is unchanging and eternal, how to reconcile this statement of the Buddha? Rather than considering the possibility that a great, awakened soul such as Buddha could be mistaken, I decided that I must consider more deeply what actual meaning he is attaching to the word "consciousness" in this statement of his, because it seems that everything hinges on knowing his actual implication.

It would seem that those who say there can be no Eternal Principle, (because all is empty) are refuted by none other than Nagarjuna himself, when he states that while it is foolish to believe in phenomena as self-existent, it is even crazier to think that "emptiness" *(shunyata)* is real. The missing key here is that emptiness is an idea that can only be applied to objects. It cannot be applied to the purely abstract, which is an Eternal Principle, and thus cannot be said to be an object. It cannot even be considered as an object of Knowledge, for it is Knowledge itself, beyond all dichotomy of subject and object.

Yet the *Uttaratantra Shastra* makes it very clear that Buddha Nature is such an unchanging Eternal Principle. Logically, a Buddhist who would deny an Eternal Principle must deny even Buddha Nature. But in the absence of Buddha Nature, how could anything be known at all? Obviously, none of these assertions could be made to begin with, without a "Knower."

Still, there is the question of "Eternalism." What was meant by Buddha when he said that "consciousness" is not eternal? If his statement were understood according to a nihilistic interpretation, it would seem that in denying an Eternal Principle, then, by logical extension, he would also be denying his own ability to know anything. Without such capacity, how could he make any assertions at all? It is more reasonable to assume that by "consciousness" the Buddha means awareness *(Rigpa)*, which has, within a context of waking, dream, and dreamless sleep states, apparently divided itself into subject and object. Of course, the Vedanta would agree that these states are real only from the relative standpoint, and impermanent. They have as their foundation Avidya/Ignorance, also called *Marigpa* within Tibetan Buddhism.

It is telling that the word "consciousness" contains the prefix "con," meaning "with," or "beside," thereby implying awareness in a dual mode. The word "awareness" has no such connotation. Perhaps this is why some think it more accurately descriptive of the Unitive Principle, than the inherently dualistic term, "consciousness."

Decidedly, then, it is an unfortunate mistake not to take into account the subtle connotation of this word. Of course, we know that what a Vedantist implies by that word, ultimately, has nothing whatsoever to do with dualism. Still, it seems understandable to me why some Buddhists mistakenly believe that Vedanta is dualistic to some degree. They do not understand that Vedantists do not use that word in the same sense that Buddhists understand it. The implication is entirely different than what they take it to be. And if the idea of "Rigpa" is taken into consideration, then the implication is precisely the same as that of the Vedanta. For the Vedantist, Consciousness is Turiya, connoting a simple, undivided awareness beyond the states of waking, dreaming, and deep sleep. As my guru often says in this regard: "Your Buddha is my Siva; your emptiness, my Samadhi, Your Prajnaparam, my Brahman."

Please, take it Personally

Now there is the issue of Atheism and Theism. Buddhism and Hinduism both contain stages of the path, teachings that conform to ideas of relative and absolute truth. Both Shankara and Nagarjuna concur on this. In either path, until one has realized the Highest — Brahman or *Prajna Param* — some utilization of relative truth is necessary for progress to be made. This is called a provisional teaching. Worship of the personal God may be a relative truth compared with nondual realization of the Absolute Brahman, but it is an absolutely necessary stage for most all beings. How many are truly ready or even capable of fully cognizing or surrendering to the purely abstract? Until we have become stronger, we still need something tangible to hold onto. Even in Tibetan Buddhism there are the creation and completion stages in which one progresses from visualizing the deity as being outside oneself, to visualizing oneself as the deity, and then finally allowing even that subtle form to pass away in the vast expanse of the infinite, ineffable light of Awareness.

I have heard it said that Atheism means that what I worship is external to myself. I can accept that. But it must also be admitted that Theism in Vedanta is a provisional teaching which leads the aspirant step by step toward the nontheism implied by the great statement *"Tat tvam asi"* (That thou art), in which subject and object, worshiper and worshiped, etc., pass away and only the One remains. Of course, one would still delight in tasting the nectar of devotion to the Personal God too.

Clarifying Outlook of Swami Vivekananda

With all this talk about emptiness, and voidism, of nihilism, etc., the following words by Swami Vivekananda, excerpted from the discourse, "God in Everything," in the book, *Jnana Yoga*, should clarify the quintessential Vedantic perspective:

"....he who is carried along by his heart alone has to undergo many ills, for now and then he is liable to tumble into pitfalls. The combination of the heart and head is what we want. I do not mean that a man should compromise his heart for his brain or vice versa, but let everyone have an infinite amount of heart and feeling, and at the same time an infinite amount of reason. Is there any limit to what we want in this world? Is not the world infinite? There is room for an infinite amount of feeling, and also for an infinite amount of culture and reason. Let them come together without limit, let them be running together, as it were, in parallel lines, each with the other.

Most of the religions understand this fact, but the error into which they all seem to fall is the same: they are carried away by the heart, the feelings. There is evil in the world, give up the world: that is the great teaching, and the only teaching, no doubt. Give up the world. There cannot be two opinions that to understand the truth every one of us has to give up error. There cannot be two opinions that to understand the Truth every one of us in order to be good must give up evil; there cannot be two opinions that everyone of us, to have life, must give up what is death.

And yet, what remains to us if this theory involves giving up the life of the senses, life as we know it? And what else do we mean by life? If we give this up, what remains?

We shall understand this better when, later on, we come to the more philosophical portions of Vedanta. But for the present I beg to state that in Vedanta alone we find a rational solution of the problem. Here I can only lay before you what Vedanta seeks to teach; and that is the deification of the world. Vedanta does not in reality denounce the world. The ideal of renunciation nowhere attains such a height as in the teachings of Vedanta. But, at the same time, dry suicidal advice is not intended; it really means deification of the world — giving up the world as we think of it, as we know it, as it appears to us — and to know what it really is. Deify it; it is God alone. We read at the commencement of one of the oldest of the Upanisad: 'Whatever exists in this universe is to be covered with the Lord.'

We have to cover everything with the Lord Himself, not by a false sort of optimism, not by blinding our eyes to evil, but by really seeing God in everything. Thus we have to give up the world, and when the world is given up, what remains? God. What is meant? You can have your wife, it does not mean that you are to abandon her; but you are to see God in your wife. Give up your children; what does that mean? To turn them out of doors, as some human brutes do in every country? Certainly not. That is diabolism; it is not religion. But see God in your children. So in everything. In life and in death, in happiness and in misery, the Lord is equally present. The whole world is full of the Lord. Open your eyes and see Him.

This is what Vedanta teaches. Give up the world which you have conjectured, because your conjecture was based upon a very partial experience, upon very poor reasoning, and upon your own weakness. Give it up. The world we have been thinking of so long, the world to which we have been clinging to so long, is a false world of our own creation. Give that up. Open your eyes and see that, as such, it never existed; it was a dream, maya. What existed was the Lord Himself. It is He who is in the child, in the wife, and in the husband; it is He who is in the good and in the bad. He is in the sin and in the sinner; He is in life and in death.

A tremendous assertion indeed! Yet that is the theme which the Vedanta wants to demonstrate, to teach, and to preach. This is just the opening theme."

Taking this vision and applying it to our own western culture and religion, we see that although the Bible verse, *"The earth is the Lord's and the fullness thereof"* is couched in dualistic language, I cannot help but think that it is not meant to be understood in the dual sense. The "earth" is the "Lord's" seems to imply a distinction between creator and creation, between creator and creature. Yet this distinction is more like a "line drawn on water," as Sri Ramakrishna has said, for the implication of the

very same verse is qualified by the word "fullness," suggesting a homogeneity and pervasiveness that blurs such distinction, implying a common identity. It is what the rishis of India called *Purnyata* — Full!

So the inner meaning, the true spirit of this verse, is precisely the same as Swami Vivekananda's exquisite expression of monistic Truth: *"The whole world is full of the Lord. Open your eyes and see Him."* I love how Swamiji further resolves the question of duality so simply, so directly, and with such finality: *"What existed was the Lord Himself."* Here, his denial of Absolute Reality for the empirically-valid world of sense experience never approaches the extreme of nihilism, for he does not deny Reality Itself, only the unreal world that, through ignorance, we project to veil that Reality. *Sarvosmi* — Existence is. It never is not. In ascribing true existence to this world of changing and therefore impermanent forms, we delude ourselves. For the scriptures state that what is nonexistent in the "beginning" and also nonexistent in the "end," cannot rationally be considered to exist in the "middle" (manifestation) either. In a sense, we allow mere appearances to become our false idol, although God alone is always and ever the Existence Absolute, the Consciousness Absolute, and the Bliss Absolute. Is this not what is implied also by the Jewish prophet when he stated, *"Hear O Israel! The Lord our God is One."*

Perhaps the non-dualist (of whatever cultural religious tradition) who wishes to transcend this false mental superimposition that he may better perceive Divine Reality, is the ultimate iconoclast, or "idol-breaker." But he breaks his own idol, which is the idol of external, false appearance, that he may know the true Lord and Mother, which is pure, divine Essence. And he breaks but his own idols, not those of others, for he understands that all must come to understanding in their own time, and more often than not, pass through that phase in which nature's transformations seem the more immediate reality.

And further, once he sees the Reality that the symbols imply, what were previously idols then cease to be idols and instead become sources of illumination, lenses which direct our attention to what is true. As understanding grows, it is seen that forms were never real "as such," in that their appearance is not self-produced or self-arising, but rather, is dependent upon a basis which is God alone.

So like in that common Vedantic metaphor of the snake in the rope, the snake may never have existed in the true sense of the word, yet it could not have been perceived in the first place in the absence of the rope. Adherents of the philosophy of Kashmir Shaivism take the position that the world (the snake) is perfectly real, in the sense that its basis, or Shiva (the rope), is real, and in fact, Reality Itself. Even accepting the truth of their insight, the theory of Maya is not contradicted or shown to be false, for the appearing forms can still be said to be unreal in that they come and go and are impermanent. *"Therefore bear them patiently, oh Arjuna,"* says Sri Krishna in the Bhagavad Gita.

Only Renunciation is Fearless

It may only be natural that we take the world to be real, given the insistent and persistent nature of sense experience. It may be natural for the child, in testing the boundaries of its experience of the world, to place its hand in fire, and then just

Vivekananda in Chicago at the Parliament of Religions

as natural, upon experiencing firsthand the truth of cause and effect, to refrain from doing so again. Just so, once we experience the unsatisfactory nature of samsara for ourselves, it is perfectly natural to give up this mayic world, whose true nature we have mistaken by our own imperfect conjecture. *"As such, it never existed. What existed was the Lord Himself."* For matter is like a membrane that must be pierced in order that we may emerge from our prakritika womb into that greater life in which all live, move, and have their existence. The conception of matter as self-existent must be discarded in favor of immersion in the *"Magna Mater,"* or the Great Mother.

The external aspect of Prakriti can be likened to the church that Swami Vivekananda spoke of. He said, in the interest of broad-mindedness, that *"It is good to be born in a church, but not to die in one."* Metaphorically speaking, to die in that "church" implies that we do not strive to free ourselves from the narrowness of identification with matter and thereby continue to be dragged *"from birth to death, and death to birth,"* as he wrote. To broaden our perspective beyond the confines of that church means that we are no longer "sectarian." Our sense of identity has outgrown the "I," the particular, and come to rest in "Thou," the universal. In that "universal church" we find identity with all, for we know that substratum which is common to all.

These are some ideas that have occurred to me in response to Swamiji's penetrating insights. His words need so much more reflection. I know I will never plumb the depth or fathom them completely. The meanings inherent in them are endless, so much is there to be discovered. His words are living scripture, like expressions of that creative Word or transcendental Veda. It is so inspiring to see the infinite knowledge that gets reflected in the purified mind of such a one.

The Awakening continued from page 55

absolute world — a world of unfading beauty, eternal purity, and perennial source of joy.

So Sri Ramakrishna is an ideal guru, an ideal teacher. He never wanted that we should pay any kind of exclusive reverence to him. And when he spoke about Nirvikalpa Samadhi, he spoke from his own personal experience. But the greatest gift of Sri Ramakrishna is bhava mukha. He did not stay in Nirvikalpa Samadhi. If one stays in Nirvikalpa Samadhi he cannot teach people, cannot help people.

That is why Sri Ramakrishna resisted the temptation of merging, and said to Divine Mother, "Mother, don't make me a brahmajnani." That means don't make me ascend the topmost height of realization, for then I will not be able to teach people. So the Divine Mother said, then stay in bhava mukha. The Bhava mukha state means you see the manifestation of God as well as God as a principle. In the bhava mukha state Sri Ramakrishna became an ideal teacher. Bhava mukha state is a state of I-consciousness connected with the personal God, called the Divine Mother. So in that state of consciousness, Sri Ramakrishna gave illumination on the first of January to the householder devotees.

God comes to raise the consciousness of human beings to a level where God will be real and the world of appearance will disappear from the mind of the individual. This is the awakening of power. The awakening of power that I am talking about is possible for every individual if he's got a tremendous urge to realize God with determination, with enthusiasm, with purity of mind, and with longing of the heart. And if this longing of the heart becomes extreme, God, who is the Antaryami, the Inner Ruler Immortal seated in the Heart, will remove all his obstacles and make the mortal, immortal. Man will be then called a jivanmukta. And that jivanmukta, an illumined man, will be a treasure to whatever civilization he may belong to.

Paravasta Sam Bailey has been a devout student of Vedanta and Babaji Bob Kindler since 1994. A serious practitioner of religion, he previously took hand in the Sufi Ruhaniat Order and also studied Essene Nazirite Christianity to become an ordained Essene minister.

Swami Aseshananda, a direct disciple of Sri Sarada Devi, Sri Ramakrishna's wife and spiritual consort, was the Spiritual Minister of the Vedanta Society of Portland for over forty years. He also received holy company with some of the direct disciples of the Great Master. He is the author of Glimpses of a Great Soul, on the life and teachings of Swami Saradananda.

NECTAR BOOK REVIEWS

Mahendra Nath Gupta
Recorder of the Gospel
by Swami Chetanananda
Vedanta Society of St Louis, 2011
Paperback, 590 pgs.

Mahendra Nath Gupta, known as "M." in the Gospel of Sri Ramakrishna, was a modern day householder rishi (sage), an educator, and a true disciple. As the recorder of Sri Ramakrishna's conversations, his own life and that of Sri Ramakrishna's are intimately entwined. M. sat for five years with his master and then spent the next 50 years sharing and assimilating that great impression on his life and mind, becoming a man of steady wisdom who spoke only of God. He himself became proof of Ramakrishna's statement to a few close disciples: *"He who thinks of me will attain my wealth, as children inherit their parents' wealth. My wealth is: knowledge, devotion, discrimination, renunciation, pure love, and Samadhi."*

Swami Chetanananda's beautifully designed and organized biography on M. is graced with translations of material previously only available in Bengali that show the deep relationship he had with Swami Vivekananda and Holy Mother, portions of the Kathamrita (original Bengali form of the Gospel) that were not translated into English, as well as reminiscences of M. by over 20 persons. Not only do we get a rare view into the inner workings of the Guru-disciple relationship, we watch a householder (which most of us are), who had all the attendant challenges of spouse, children, and work, transform into a sage who transmitted the spirit of his guru's wealth as listed above.

In the chapter entitled "An Ideal Householder Devotee," the author assembles M.'s record of Sri Ramakrishna's teachings to householders. Many of the daily issues and choices householders deal with are touched upon, showing Sri Ramakrishna's unbounded sympathy for the plight of aspiring householders. Of particular note, this section also shows how Sri Ramakrishna handled M.'s desire to enter monastic life due to his increasing spirit of renunciation and longing for realization. As his guru instructed, M. remained in the world like a servant who only serves others. As the author points out, Sri Ramakrishna once told him, "Divine Mother binds the [teacher of scripture] to the world with one tie; otherwise, who would remain to explain the sacred book?"

Though well-known as the humble amanuensis of Sri Ramakrishna, seldom do people discover his stature as an educator. The chapter on "The Morton Institution and Naimisharanya" is inspirational reading for all who desire a holistic approach to education. In this era where the lack of human values is noticeably missing from our educational systems, where fear of religious fundamentalism and control disallows a spiritual or transcendent perspective on human life in public schools, and the purpose of education is connected with consumerism, wealth, power, and pleasure (i.e. selfishness), the astute teachings and methods of Mahendranath Gupta are a dose of sanity. He states, *"One should know first the contents of human beings, and then have a philosophy or the plan of education. Each human being has three bodies: gross or physical, subtle or intellectual, and causal or spiritual. It is extremely important to feed all three bodies so that they become strong. Our schools and colleges are feeding only the subtle body. The educational system must be connected with the spiritual body, which will form character and will bring peace and joy. If education is not connected with the Highest Ideal, the moral character will not be strong."*

A biography of M. is necessarily a history of the Gospel: its beginnings in M.'s experiences and training with Sri Ramakrishna, its development in the form of M.'s personal diaries, and finally its presentation in the five volumes of the Kathamrita, later translated as the Gospel. It is sometimes mentioned that Sri Ramakrishna's special teachings on the glory of renunciation and the life of the sannyasin (monk) are not in the Gospel since he did not give those out when householders were present. However, it is also true that the publication of the Gospel became the inspiration of countless young men joining the Ramakrishna Order as monks. Swami Chetanananda also gives the following quote by a monk who spent time with M.: *"He would paint in brilliant colors the life of the sadhu [monk], his great ideal and mission in life, his great sacrifice for the highest end, and would show infinite regret if any sannyasin [monk] neglected his rare opportunity of realizing the summum bonum of life. Sadhus learned from him the glory of their mission."*

This new biography of M. is highly recommended. Readers will not fail to imbibe the spirit of Truth, sincerity, earnestness, devotion to God and guru, and renunciation that saturated the life of Mahendra Nath Gupta.

Annapurna Sarada

Children of Immortal Bliss
by Paul Hourihan
Vedanta Shores Press, 2008
Paperback, 208 pgs.

"Is man a tiny boat in a tempest, raised one moment on the foamy crest of a billow and dashed down into a yawning chasm the next, rolling to and fro at the mercy of good and bad actions? Is there no hope? Is there no escape? — was

the cry that went up from the bottom of the heart of despair. It reached the throne of mercy, and words of hope and consolation came down and inspired a Vedic sage, and he stood up before the world and in trumpet voice proclaimed the glad tidings: 'Hear, ye children of immortal bliss! Even ye that reside in higher spheres! I have found the Ancient One, who is beyond all darkness, all delusion: knowing Him alone you shall be saved from death over again.'"

This bold exhortation by Swami Vivekananda, spoken at the Chicago Parliament of Religions, was itself inspired by a passage in the Svetasvatara Upanishad which begins, "Hear, O children of immortal bliss, You are born to be united with the Lord."

Paul Hourihan, the author of *"Children of Immortal Bliss,"* has himself heard this call to realize that blessed state where the spiritual aspirant attains complete absorption in Brahman. Mr. Hourihan was a student of Swami Ritananda, a monk of the Ramakrishna Order. This illumined introduction to Vedanta not only covers the essential foundational teachings of this sublime philosophy, but articulates these teachings in a uniquely accessible fashion. Beginning students will appreciate the heartfelt clarity and contemporary sensibility with which the author not only explains but also transmits these ancient teachings.

More advanced students will find this book a joy to read as well. Though the material may be familiar, these great pearls of wisdom are eternally illuminating and the depth of the author's personal sadhana inspires fresh contemplation.

Organized into four parts, *"Children of Immortal Bliss"* includes an overview of Indian mysticism, the Upanishads, Brahman, and the universality of spiritual traditions.

Such teachings as the gunas, the fourfold mind, karma and desire, Brahman, mantra, maya, and the Self, among others are presented from the point of view of one who has undergone serious sadhana under an illumined teacher and has gained genuine strength and peace due to the practical application of this philosophy. Mr. Hourihan was also an academic scholar with a Ph.D. in literature, and this accounts for the clear analytical framework upon which he builds this spiritually uplifting guide for realizing our true identity.

The chapter on Brahman contains a particularly skilful evocation of Brahman as emptiness, or void. This difficult and abstruse teaching is unwrapped in language familiar to the Western mind while preserving the integrity of the tradition.

The final chapter called "Truth is One" focuses on several outstanding individual mystics from different traditions. Plotinus, Lao Tsu, Meister Eckhart, and Rumi are invoked as spiritual giants with particular viewpoints who were unique and at the same time shared an underlying universal vision of the immortality of the Soul, unconditioned and infinite, without beginning or end.

This introduction to fundamental Vedanta truths will serve to inspire the reader to realize and make these truths his or her own.

Anurag Neal Aronowitz

Maya Yoga
by Keith Dowman
Vajra Publications, 2010
Paperback, 112 pgs.

Maya Yoga — Longchenpa's Finding Comfort and Ease in Enchantment — is the most recent offering from Keith Dowman, author-translator of fourteen books in the Tantric Buddhist tradition. Long regarded as an insightful translator of sacred texts, he has since 1966 been a practitioner of the Tibetan Vajrayana. A partial list of Dowman's illustrious teachers includes Kanjur Rinpoche, Dudjom Rinpoche, and Namkhai Norbu Rinpoche.

Maya Yoga is Dowman's translation of the concluding volume of Longchenpa's Trilogy of *Finding Comfort and Ease* (Tibetan - Ngalso Kor Sum). All three volumes were originally translated in the mid-1970s by the late Buddhist scholar Herbert Guenther. Whereas Dr. Guenther called this third book "Wonderment," Dowman has chosen to name it "Maya Yoga," intimating the realization of awakening (yoga) in the midst of the enchantment (maya) in which we all find ourselves enmeshed.

Longchen Rabjam (1308-1364), usually referred to as Longchenpa, is one of the most brilliant teachers in the history of Tibetan Buddhism. A prolific writer and major force in the Nyingma (original) Tibetan Buddhist tradition, he systematized the teachings of that lineage in his Seven Treasures compilation and wrote extensively on the view, meditation, and action of Dzogchen. The English translation of Dzogchen, Great Perfection, is sometimes rendered as Great Completion. Dzogchen is also called ati yoga (highest yoga) and is the ultimate spiritual approach of the Nyingma tradition, which traces its origins to the 7th century (CE) Indian mahasiddha Padmasambhava.

In his introduction, Dowman presents Longchenpa's view of the nature of the enchantment of maya, which assumes two aspects: *"The first is the basic immaculate maya that is our original, natural state of being.... The second aspect is the delusory maya created by the intellect, known as the maya of false conception."* Expanding these two fundamental aspects Longchenpa presents a detailed fourfold view:

> In that space of uncreated magical creation
> the actual show that is the basis of transformation,
> the polluted show that is to be disinfected,
> the technical show of skilful decontamination,
> and the ultimate show of primal awareness —
> these four are mere instances of magic show.

– continued on page 64

SRV Associations — Babaji's Teaching Schedule 2012

Major Holy Days, Classes, Retreats, and Pilgrimages
(Jai Ma Concerts, Children's Classes, & other events — to be announced on SRV's Website)

Jan/Feb 2012

SRV San Francisco (Meditation, 6 to 7am)
- 1/20 Fri 7:00pm Arati/Satsang
- 1/21 Sat 9:30am Class: Svetasvataropanisad
-           7:00pm **Vivekananda/Brahmananda Puja**
- 1/22 Sun 9:30am Class: Svetasvataropanisad
- 1/23 Mon 7:00pm Arati/Satsang
- 1/24 Tue 7:00pm Arati/Satsang

SRV Oregon (Meditation, 6 to 7am - Call to confirm)
- 1/28 Sat 9:30am Class: Svetasvataropanisad
-           6:00pm **Sri Sarasvati/Sarada Puja**
- 1/29 Sun 9:30am Class: Svetasvataropanisad
- 2/1 Wed 7:00pm Scripture Class with Anurag
- 2/3 Fri 7:00pm Satsang with Babaji
- 2/4 Sat 9:30am Class: Svetasvataropanisad
-           6:00pm SRV Puja
- 2/5 Sun 9:30am Class: Svetasvataropanisad
- 2/8 Wed 7:00pm Scripture Class with Anurag
- 2/10 Fri 7:00pm Satsang with Babaji

SRV Weekend Seminar at Portland Ashram
Friday pm, Feb 10th – Sunday noon, Feb 12th
Subject: Dissolving the Mindstream in Meditation

April/May 2012

SRV San Francisco (Meditation, 6 to 7am)
- 4/20 Fri 7:00pm Arati/Satsang
- 4/21 Sat 9:30am Class: Svetasvataropanisad
-           7:00pm SRV Puja
- 4/22 Sun 9:30am Class: Svetasvataropanisad
- 4/23 Mon 7:00pm Arati/Satsang
- 4/24 Tues 7:00pm Arati/Satsang

SRV Oregon (Meditation, 6 to 7am - Call to confirm)
- 4/28 Sat 9:30am Class: Svetasvataropanisad
-           6:00pm **Shankara Advaita Puja**
- 4/29 Sun 9:30am Class: Svetasvataropanisad
- 5/2 Wed 7:00pm Scripture Class with Anurag
- 5/4 Fri 7:00pm Satsang with Babaji
- 5/5 Sat 9:30am Class: Svetasvataropanisad
-           6:00pm SRV Puja
- 5/6 Sun 9:30am Class: **The Four Noble Truths**
- 5/9 Wed 7:00pm Scripture Class with Anurag

SRV Mother's Day Spring Retreat!
Thursday, May 10th – Sunday, May 13th
Subject: The Teachings of Yoga Vasishtha
Location: TBA

June/July 2012

SRV San Francisco (Meditation, 6 to 7am)
- 6/30 Sat 9:30am Class: Svetasvataropanisad
-           7:00pm SRV Puja
- 7/1 Sun 9:30am Class: Svetasvataropanisad

SRV's Summer Retreat on the American River
Gurupurnima & Swami Vivekananda's Mahasamadhi
Tues, July 3rd (pm) – Tuesday, July 10th (noon)
Subject: Vivekananda & True Freedom
For more information call SRV Office: 808-990-3354

SRV Oregon (Meditation, 6 to 7am - Call to confirm)
- 7/14 Sat 9:30am Class: Svetasvataropanisad
-           6:00pm SRV Puja
- 7/15 Sun 9:30am Class: Svetasvataropanisad
- 7/18 Wed 7:00pm Scripture Class with Anurag
- 7/20 Fri 7:00pm Satsang with Babaji
- 7/21 Sat 9:30am Class: Svetasvataropanisad
-           6:00pm SRV Puja
- 7/22 Sun 9:30am Class: Svetasvataropanisad

India Pilgrimage
December/January 2012-13
Kolkata / Joyrambati / Kamarpukur
& Visit to Jungle Reserve in Bihar
Inquire via email at: srvinfo@srv.org

SRV Oregon
Portland Center:
P.O. Box 14012
Portland, OR 97293
Ph: 503-774-2410

SRV San Francisco
Healing Center:
465 Brussels Street
San Francisco, CA 94134
Ph: 415-468-4680

SRV Associations — Babaji's Teaching Schedule 2012 (continued)

*Schedule subject to change; check our website Calendar or contact your local SRV Center:
Hawaii & Oregon: 808.990.3354 – San Francisco: 415.468.4680

SRV's Autumn Retreat
Thur., October 4th – Sunday, October 7th
(Arrive Thursday night, depart Sunday pm)
Subject: Divine Mother Wisdom
Location: TBA
For more information call SRV Office, 808-990-3354

October 2012

SRV Oregon (Meditation, 6 to 7am - Call to confirm)
- 10/12 Fri 7:00pm Arati/Satsang
- 10/13 Sat 9:30am Class: TBA
- 6:00pm SRV Puja
- 10/14 Sun 9:30am Class: TBA
- 10/17 Wed 7:00pm Scripture Class with Anurag
- 10/20 Sat 9:30am Class: TBA
- 6:00pm **Durga Puja**
- 10/21 Sun 9:30am Class: TBA

SRV San Francisco (Meditation, 6 to 7 am)
- 10/26 Fri 7:00pm Satsang with Babaji
- 10/27 Sat 9:30am Class: TBA
- 7:00pm **Durga Puja**
- 10/28 Sun 9:30am Class: TBA
- 10/29 Mon 7:00pm Arati/Satsang
- 10/30 Tues 7:00pm Arati/Satsang

Spiritual Classes for Children

Contact Annapurna Sarada — Phone 808-990-3354

SRV Hawai'i Administrative Office:
PO Box 1364
Honoka'a, HI 96727
Ph: 808-990-3354

SRV Associations' website:
www.srv.org
email:
srvinfo@srv.org

Join the SRV Facebook Group. Contact jamiji@gmail.com

 ## Big Island of Hawaii

SRV Hawai'i
Babaji's Teaching Schedule

Sundays, 2:30 - 5:30pm
Rotating locations, directions: 808-990-3354

Feb / Mar / April 2012
Dissolving the Mindstream in Yoga
February 26
March 4, 11, 18, 25
April 1, 8

May / June 2012
Teachings from Yoga Vasishtha
May 27
June 3, 10, 17, 24

Aug / Sep 2012
Nondual Wisdom of Vedanta
August 5, 12, 19, 26
September 2, 9, 16, 23

Nov / Dec 2012
Tantra & Vedanta - The Two Great Streams
November 11, 18, 25
December 2, 9, 16, 23

Schedule subject to change.
Check www.srv.org for Hawaii retreats

Stay connected
through our website: www.srv.org

Sign up for:
- SRV e-Newsletter: Mundamala, published quarterly
- SRV Magazine: Nectar of Non-Dual Truth
- Raja Yoga email study on Yoga Sutras with Babaji
- SRV's Facebook page
- SRV's YouTube channel: Teaching videos with Babaji
- Godblogs: Inspired Dialog

Book Reviews continued from page 61

All form (maya) arises out of the ineffable emptiness of pure potential (shunyata). The Prajnaparamita Hridaya Sutra (Heart Sutra) states: "Form is emptiness; emptiness is form." At the level of non-conceptual awareness these appearances are pure expressions of the nature of mind. This is what Longchenpa refers to as "the actual show." However, from this pure appearance the dichotomizing intellect imposes dualities such as "us and them," "like and dislike," and so on. This is the "polluted show" of samsara to be disinfected. "The technical show of skilful decontamination" is the vast array of spiritual practices — all of them ultimately illusory as well.

"Longchenpa's fourth functional aspect (the ultimate show) is the maya of primordially pure pristine awareness. This is indistinguishable from the basic immaculate maya. It arises with complete ego-loss and surrender, and it subverts all sense of distinction between subjective inner and objective outer perception." In truth, the apparent goal and the starting point are not different in essence; it is only maya (the magical display) that makes them seem so.

Longchenpa uses eight analogies to elucidate this enchanting display of samsara's magical illusion. These analogies were first compiled by Nagarjuna, the famous Buddhist founder of the Madhyamaka school, who lived sometime between 150 - 250 CE. Longchenpa poetically presents these analogies — dream, magic show, optical illusion, mirage, reflection of the moon in water, echo, a city of gandharvas, and apparition — from the view of the Great Perfection. In the first of his book's two appendices, Dowman offers us two more analogies in the style of Longchenpa — the motion picture and the hologram. He suggests that both Nagarjuna and Longchenpa would have found these modern phenomena to be suitable analogies to examine our collective bewitchment. Dowman's two poems possess the same lucid quality and directness of Longchenpa's verse.

In addition to his expert translations, long admired among Tantric Buddhists, the introductions and appendices Dowman writes for his translations are highly regarded for their clarity and insight. This is testament to his many years of practice with and blessings from some of the greatest lamas of the Tibetan diaspora. The introduction to *Maya Yoga* comprises half of this slim, but potent volume of Dzogchen precepts. The rhythm of Dowman's own writing is like the voice of an old friend guiding us through the flashing summits and gentle expanses of the great Longchenpa's vision.

D.S. Lokanath

Indian Thought and its Development
by Albert Schweitzer
Beacon Press, Boston, 1957
Hard cover, 272 pgs.

Whatever high regard I had previously held or evinced for Albert Schweitzer due to the general assessment of western civilization about his greatness took a serious nose dive upon encountering this book. Like a deaf and dumb mute who should never have attempted to describe his first taste of ice cream, just so, this "great man" of the West should never have undertaken to explain Indian thought and philosophy, especially under the

unreliable surface mantle of a mere historical retrospective.

Schweitzer calls into question his own historical perspective, as well as his supposed universal ideology, by claiming that India and its great luminaries were all inspired mainly by the *"Christian God of Love,"* when the fact of the matter is that India was producing spiritual giants by the scores while Christianity was still an infant. According to him, even the great contemporary lights of Mother India such as Rammohan Roy, Mahatma Gandhi, Sri Ramakrishna, Swami Vivekananda, and Sri Aurobindo, were all made greater when they got influenced by the *"higher ethics and morals of Christianity."* Even those who are at least aware of England's embarrassing encounter with Mahatma Gandhi in the past century would know better than this, as history has already proven which of these two — Christian England or Hindu India — held the higher moral ground in the matter.

Schweitzer was known for criticizing the tenets of his own church and religion, thereby showing some objectivity and impartiality. But acceptance of the faiths of others, not conversionary tactics, is the real key to Universality. Narrowness under the guise of Universality is an old and oft-repeated story. One may profess to love all of humanity, and propose the equality of mankind, various cultures, and different religions, yet at the same time never really leave the confines of one's own preferred spiritual ideal, considering it to be superior to all others. This very narrowness was found by this reader in many of the pages of this book, contradictions which only underscore the vast difference between an altruist or theologian, and an illumined soul.

Illumined souls and spiritual masters like Sri Ramakrishna and Swami Vivekananda were the possessors of inner peace, not wagers of war against other countries. Had Albert Sweitzer lived to the present millennia to see this Christian nation posing as friend to all while marching across the borders of other lands in search of resources in the mode of war-waging soldiers armed to the teeth with nuclear-tipped messengers, he might have changed his tune. For ahimsa, nonviolence, has always been at the basis of Indian thought and philosophy — a fact that he obviously overlooked in his assessment of India, along with a host of other eternal, nondual axioms of Indian Philosophy.

Schweitzer, along with most westerners, does not understand monks, much less sannyasins. This is evidenced in his short-sighted assessment of Vivekananda. While admitting the great swami's excellent works and admirable qualities, he betrays himself in his hasty summation that Vivekananda indulged in *"hard, unjust, and contradictory judgements."* About the spiritual side of Ramakrishna and Vivekananda, he concludes that they both *"drew their final criterion for the judgement of spiritual matters from ethical thought."* But can matters truly spiritual ever be judged by either ethics or thought? Is it not the other way around? This topsy-turvy way of seeing is typical of the western mind.

Babaji Bob Kindler

www.ingramcontent.com/pod-product-compliance
Lightning Source LLC
Chambersburg PA
CBHW081126080526
44587CB00021B/3768